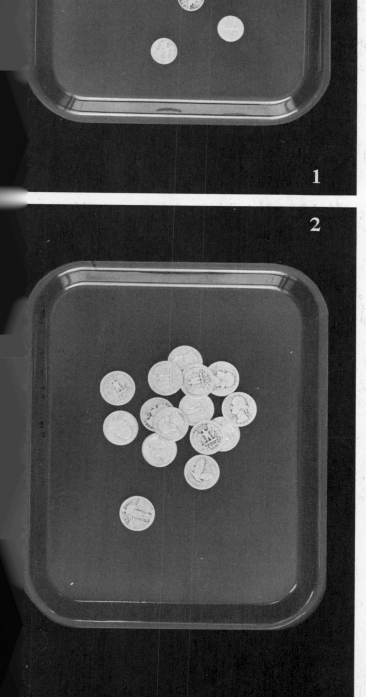

1

2

More succinctly than several thousand words, the pictures on these pages explain the meaning of this book. The plates shown here belonged to two hatcheck girls, named for the purpose of this story Mary and Jane, who both worked in the same booth in a downtown restaurant. One day Mary placed a dime on her plate as a decoy to entice tips from her customers, and Jane followed suit, but instead she put a quarter on hers.

TWO HOURS LATER

Jane collected two and a half times more in tips than her partner. She used salesmanship. She knew that sometimes a picture symbol—in this case a silver coin—speaks more eloquently than words. And more effectively.

She put Visual Persuasion into practice.

Do you?

McGraw-Hill Book Company, Inc. / New York Toronto London 1961

Visual Persuasion

written and designed by / Stephen Baker

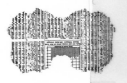

America is the most visual-minded nation in the world. Picture-talk is all around us. The pragmatic approach to evaluating art. Skepticism of anything aesthetic. Demand for realism. The average American's lack of confidence in his "good taste." His hunger for culture. What about future prospects?

The "girl next door" is the best saleswoman advertisers have. Exit the frozen-faced damsel, enter the gal-pal. Versatility of top photographic models. The changing shape of the ideal woman. The popularity of the Rheingold Girl. The "new look" in male models. Nonprofessional professionals. Should models be young, old, tall, short, blondes, brunettes?

Seeing is a state of mind. Pictures can be explained rationally, but their deepest impact is on the subconscious. Latent meanings of shapes, textures, symbols. Objects have genders, too. What creates optical illusions? The psychology of type faces. It is the total impression that counts. Eye movements are based on conditioned reflexes. The importance of "mood" in an illustration. There is more to color than meets the eye.

Americans have mixed notions about sex. Sexual furtiveness. The power of sensual pictures in advertising. Male ideas of sex are not like those of a female; different advertising appeals are needed. Clothes make the woman. Strip tease in reverse. What gives women that provocative quality? Nudity versus seductiveness. The sex appeal of fabrics.

Hankering for the good old days. Longing for childhood—the emotional need to "go back." Can an advertiser afford to be "old-fashioned"? The charm of type faces of yesteryear. Resistance to change. Are the most valuable antiques those of the best design? Mixing "periods." The appeal of the "old order of family life."

Certain feelings are as old as mankind. How to get the reader emotionally involved with the illustration. The appeal of travel pictures. Typewriter advertising. How to make the beholder feel he owns the room he sees. Is "human interest" in furniture pictures necessary? Automobiles evoke strong emotions. The hidden forces behind every food illustration. Why "torture commercials" make viewers go out and buy pills. The funny reasons people have for looking at the funnies.

Women have feelings all their own. What they like—and what they would like to do if they had a chance. The changing role of the American woman. Is "togetherness" all right by both sexes? Do women have a sense of humor? The kind of "sex" she likes—and rejects—in illustrations. Examples of advertising that make women buy.

Is it necessary to have an image? The danger of having a "smörgasbord" image. How to find the one that suits the corporation best. Images are not built in a day. They can be changed. What is your "visual profile"? Art technique can give a company a "personality" all its own. The look of Lord & Taylor. How Titeflex, Inc., modernized its image. Outstanding image-building advertising campaigns.

A few words about industry's failure to use "visual persuasion" to its fullest advantage.

a few words of thanks to those who made thi

For anyone holding a full-time position in a major advertising agency, it would be bordering on the brink of imbecility to attempt to write a book single-handed unless he were ready to

1. lose his wife
2. be treated in a hospital for a nervous breakdown
3. produce a piece of work of no consequence

I had no intention of playing the role of the star performer in any of these adventures. My wife is angry enough with me for working at all. I am much too busy at the moment to take a rest in a sanatorium. And to write and have a book published just for the sake of being introduced at parties as an "author" hardly makes the effort worthwhile.

Visual Persuasion was researched, organized, written, and laid out by me. However, there came a time when all the pieces began to fit into a giant jigsaw puzzle, and the book began to "write itself."

I was most anxious to illustrate all major points; the subject after all calls for a pictorial treatment. For this reason I approached several photographers and illustrators, the best in their fields, and having explained the purpose of *Visual Persuasion,* asked them if they had the "right" pictures in stock for such an endeavor.

The response was gratifying. Everyone thought that *Visual Persuasion* was a "much-needed" book. Listening to the various comments made by those who should know, I very soon began to discover the reasons behind their unanimous blessing. It seems that all creative men in the business of communication have difficulties explaining the *subtle* meanings of pictures to those who buy them.

Busy as they were on other assignments, quite a few of these professionals actually prepared illustrations specially for this book. My deepest thanks to these kindred souls. I would especially like to express my gratitude to two photographers: Alfred Gescheidt and Jack Shannon. Al is one of the most brilliantly creative photographers I know, original in his ideas and impeccable in his taste. Jack is a seemingly easygoing young man (the antithesis of the stereotyped movie concept of a photographer) but so sensitive to beauty that he can hardly do wrong.

Many others share the authorship of *Visual Persuasion.* There is the large and capable research staff of Cunningham & Walsh Advertising Agency. The studies made by motivational researchers, readership inspectors, and psychologists also helped in documenting some of my own presumptions. Then there is the long and impressive list of artists and photographers whose works enliven the pages of the book: Jon Abbot, Ralph Bartholomew, Lester Beall, Richard Beatty, William Bell, Hal Berg, Lester Bookbinder, Rupert Callender, A. Devaney, June Dickson, Dirone Photography, William Duffy, Murray Duitz, Robert Ferris, Robert Frank, Steve Frankfort, Timothy Galfas, Ewing Galloway, Richard Heiman, William Helburn, William Johnston, Charles Kirk, Murray Laden, Alvin Maley, Jerry McDaniel, Rosalie, Merrihome Studios, Howard Munce, Arnold Newman, Wingate Paine, Maurice Pascal, Robert Pliskin, John Rawlings, Robert Ritta, Ben Rose (a great many photographs are his), Robert Rubic, Carl K. Shiraishi, Jacques Simson, Studio Associates, Hans Van Nes, Howard Zieff. Mention should also be made of two models: Vernice Howk and Desmond Vyfhuis.

Last but not least, my special thanks to the staff of Agency Art Studio. Under the leadership of imperturbable Sid Bahrt, they followed up much of the detail work in putting this book together, thus keeping me from going completely off my rocker.

Stephen Baker

Dedicated
to those creative men and women
who, having gathered information,
still dare to use intuition. . . .

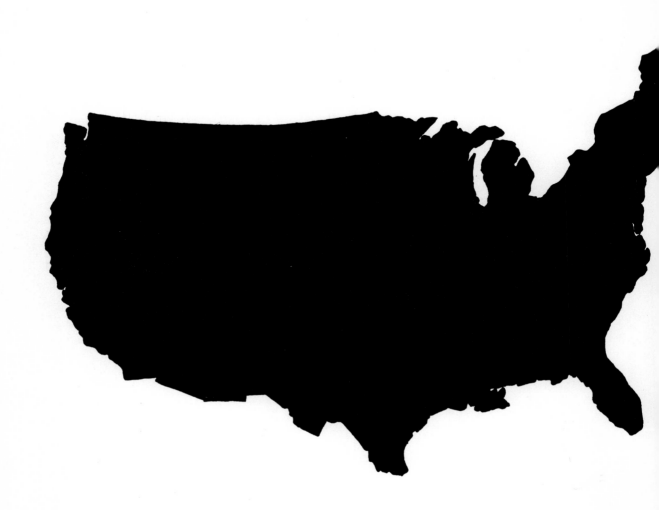

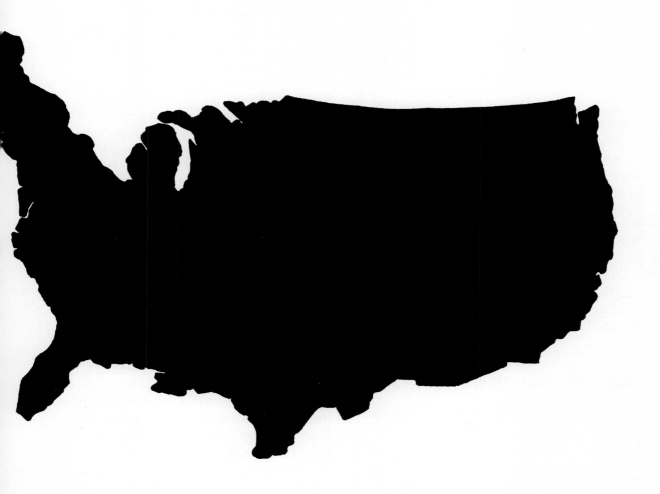

1

The peculiar taste
of the American public

America is the most visual-minded nation in the world. Never before in history have so many people received messages, day after day, by means of pictures.

It is estimated that 80 per cent of all impressions are received through the eyes. The American way of life encourages this phenomenon. There is picture-talk all around us. The average person grows so accustomed to this state of affairs that he is hardly aware of it. Ask him how he gets information. "By means of words," he will say. He is *conscious* of word communication (surveys show that most people think of "communication" as something that has to do with words). Picture communication functions on a subconscious level. It happens fast. We comprehend the messages without much effort. We hardly know what has hit us.

This makes picture communication all the more effective. The fact that pictures work subtly (and sometimes insidiously) only increases their power.

People like pictures

This is important to keep in mind when trying to understand the potency of visual communication. People don't always like words (an attitude which will be discussed later in the chapter). Because of the average person's confused feelings about words, he tends to seek out situations where all is said with pictures.

Hard to believe? Consider these facts:

In newspapers the most-read page is the comics section. Only during the war years did front-page items receive closer attention than the shenanigans of such outstanding personalities as Dick Tracy, Li'l Abner, Brenda Starr; after the war, things went back to normal. The second most-read feature in dailies is the ballooned humor panels.

The blanket coverage of the most visual medium of all, television, has become a reality; today it is possible to reach 95 per cent of the population by means of this electronic marvel. Since only 92 per cent of the people in the United States can read, books cannot do as well. The impact of shows, commercials, or anything else that happens to burst into view on the screen staggers the imagination. The average television viewer watches his set with intense concentration, though he is too embarrassed to admit this to others or to himself. Never has a mass communication medium had an audience so completely mesmerized.

Nineteen out of twenty sets are in use four hours every evening. Even more astounding is the fact that many families spend a total of fifty-six hours a week in front of the "magic box." This figure exceeds the number of hours spent in pursual of any other activity, except possibly sleep.

The impact of television in the future will, if anything, increase. Color television is slowly making a place for itself, intensifying competition with movies. In an experimental state is a video tape recorder that can be attached to sets to automatically record all desired programs when the family is away. The program can then be played back any time. Such an innovation will make it possible to rent shows from circulating libraries (set up like book libraries) and to project them on a flat wall screen (5 by 7 feet).

Picture conditioning starts early in life. Educators are discovering that the easiest way to keep their pupils' attention is by means of pictures. More and more teachers are using props (sometimes as elaborate as those in a Broadway show) to make their lectures more "interesting" to their easygoing audience. Over half a million students are receiving instruction by television. Textbooks are becoming larger, more pictorial, more colorful—and more expensive. Comics, too, have found a place for themselves in schools. Published are such picture stories as "The United Nations—And How It Works," "All about Etiquette," and "The Bible." Even IQ tests are becoming pictorial; a psychologist from Pittsburgh succeeded in devising a series of visual question–answer tests that do away with reading altogether.

Lecturers are encouraged to use "visual aids" in their talks; the mechanics of utilizing such reinforcements is now included in standard textbooks on speechmaking.

In New York an art studio specializing in the development of "pictorial" charts increased its business threefold in less than two years. Important companies go for it in a big way. A president's introductory speech at a sales meeting may often be followed by spectacles as costly as the most lavish of musicals; the nearsighted members of the audience may miss a great deal of the message, but those who are hard of hearing miss little. Even political orators, accustomed to relying exclusively on the power of the spoken word, are no longer above making use of a bit of visual wizardry. This is becoming increasingly apparent at nationally televised conventions.

There are indications that even the so-called "reading" public likes plenty of pictures. The immediate success of an all picture-caption book, the *White Collar Zoo* (on the best-seller list for several weeks), proved that the format was commercially sound. Even today, more than a hundred picture-caption books later, there seems to be room for more of the same. Buyers do not seem to tire of them.

In the magazine and newspaper field pictures help sales. *Life* magazine, the first to make lavish use of photographs, broke all precedents in its speedy climb to multimillion sales. *The Daily News*, "New York's Picture Newspaper," sells more copies than any other daily in the United States. Says wonderingly the research department at the Curtis Publishing Company: "Number of illustrations significantly influences the male (and female) reader starting the articles." This is an understatement. Pictures can invite readership where little would exist otherwise. The size of illustrations is in direct relationship with reading. Herbert Mayes, veteran editor of magazines, was keenly aware of this curious phenomenon when he took over the leadership at *McCall's*. He hardly changed the content of the publication, but he encouraged his talented art director, Otto Storch, to use the biggest pictures ever. The circulation of the magazine skyrocketed to seven million plus; for the first time since its inception it began to close in on its competitor.

Advertisers have long been aware that with larger pictures comes increased readership. The big-picture–short-copy layout has become· a staple in magazines. Over three-quarters of all ads put into print media feature pictures that take up over half the space for which the advertiser is so dearly paying.

Why does the average American prefer to receive information by means of pictures? He is not art-oriented. He distrusts aesthetics. The situation seems paradoxical, but really it is not.

Puritan tradition—the glorification of work—made our forefathers skeptical of any form of passive enjoyment, such as looking at pictures. Some of this feeling still exists today.

At the same time, pictures offer a real practical advantage to the typical American. He is usually in a hurry. Pictures present the quickest way of getting ideas across.

Pictures that communicate the fastest are usually the most effective. One major New York agency measured such effectiveness with a stop watch. Illustrations were projected to the viewer for three seconds by a special instrument, the Tachistoscope. If an illustration failed to "get through" in this time, it was put on the junk pile.

Prevalent feelings of anti-intellectualism make pictures more· acceptable than words.

American tradition prefers the "doer" rather than the "thinker." The man with a large vocabulary is viewed with mixed emotions. He is a smart guy, but can you trust him? He reads books, he is an intellectual. He is not a "man of action."

The average American learns early to rely on this kind of self-defense mechanism. He has little choice. The number of words in the English language (more than in any other) *can* be bewildering. The schools are trying to straighten out the situation, but too often they succeed only in hardening their students' subconscious resistance to words. As researcher Pierre Martineau so perceptively points out: "Rules governing words are quite rigid. They must be defined within the narrow limits to preserve mutual intelligibility of language. We are taught from early age to consider words as rigid building blocks with confined meanings. By contrast, the meaning of pictures is not hedged in and embalmed, as the teachers insist we do with words. We read whatever meaning we want to read into the picture, and do it with complete freedom. No schoolmarm or any other superior person has ever embarrassed us for 'misusing' the picture, let alone mispronouncing it or misspelling it."

"Show me"

The man-on-the-street believes what he *sees*. He prefers his own impression to that of a stranger. He instinctively mistrusts somebody else's description of an object; he would like to make up his own mind and not have a verbalizer make it up for him.

Pictures, in the opinion of the average American, offer proof positive. There is the real McCoy.

In copy research, when trying to determine audience involvement with specific ads, people talk at great length on the picture content, the art technique, the graphics of the ad—far more than they do on copy claims. They usually have strong—and vocal—opinions concerning the picture; their reactions to the text may consist of nothing more than a shrug of the shoulder.

There is no amount of advertising text that can carry the *conviction* of a photograph. Even the best description of a product-demonstration test cannot take the place of a picture taken on the scene. Testimonials of well-known people, no matter how true sounding, increase in effectiveness when accompanied by an illustration of the celebrity. There is no rational explanation for this attitude; a picture of the testifier adds no more authenticity to the message than a signature. Yet not only does readership go up if there is a picture in the ad but so does believability.

In some instances it is imperative to show an illustration in order to make a sale. Real estate agents found out a long time ago that a description of the merits of a house is not enough. The buyer wants to *see* the house (or a picture of it), count the number of windows, and check the slant of the roof all on his own. To prove various sales points a photograph is more persuasive than a drawing—but even the roughest sketch is more effective than only words.

Is it any wonder that some people think one picture is worth a thousand words?

Picture-talk—getting a message over not with words but with graphic symbols—was put to commercial use a long time ago (letters, too, evolved from pictures). Store emblems like the 200-year-old fish sign served to identify type of establishment. Today, giant manufacturers are using the same kind of device to communicate with their public. Their trade mark—a picture symbol—replaces the venerable fish sign.

Above: A classic success in its field was the poster series sponsored by "New York's Picture Newspaper," *The Daily News.* No words at all were used in getting the message across to the public, and yet—judging from the reaction—there was little difficulty in getting it across to the onlookers.

To the left: Pictures in advertisements are getting bigger. More and more magazine publishers forgo the traditional extra charge for a bleed-page ad to give advertisers maximum opportunity to use large illustrations. Says Daniel Starch in his report on a study of advertising readership: "On the average, large-illustration advertisements showed 22 per cent greater visibility on the part of men and 20 per cent on the part of women as compared with the advertisements not relying upon dominant illustrative treatment." Even more thought-provoking are the findings of Mill Shephard in his study of 36 top-ranking ads in 12 issues. He reports: "On the basis of 'remembered having seen,' 34 featured large illustrations."

The average American—more than anyone else in any other country—insists on realism in his art.

Art in this country is not judged primarily on the basis of its inherent beauty but rather on its accuracy in conveying realistic details. Thus, a portrait is "good" if it bears close resemblance to the subject. "It sure looks like him" becomes a form of the highest compliment.

Only a small child can splash colors on a canvas uninhibitedly and get away with it. The older he gets, the more he is pressed to draw realistically. Painting for the sake of expressing inner feelings and emotions is still looked upon by most Americans as an activity that should be limited only to those in need of occupational therapy.

An artist who attains skill in drawing realistically has a better chance of becoming a financial success. His paintings can even be sold to the public at large. Accurate depictors of Americana, whether pictures of cowboys breaking in horses, boys going fishing, New England landscapes, or cocker spaniels, receive considerable adoration from their fellow countrymen, who never cease to be fascinated by a display of manual dexterity. The busiest of commercial artists—Norman Rockwell, for example—have this knack. In fine art realism triumphs, too; the highest price ever paid to a living American artist was given to Andrew Wyeth for one of his photographic renderings. Even inside the walls of museums, where presumably the more artistically sophisticated people gather, it is reported that in over-the-counter sales, prints of children who look like the tots next door do much better than reproductions of Picasso's "Woman Before the Mirror"—a portrait of a damsel who made art history but one that would hardly arouse any man's romantic notions.

Typical of the kind of painting that receives approval from the collective hearts of the American public is Emanuel Leutze's exuberant conception of what Washington and his able crew looked like as they were crossing the Delaware River in 1776. Year after year thousands of visitors flock into a specially built auditorium to admire this reportorial showpiece, and almost all of them manage to confuse grandiosity of subject matter with greatness of art.

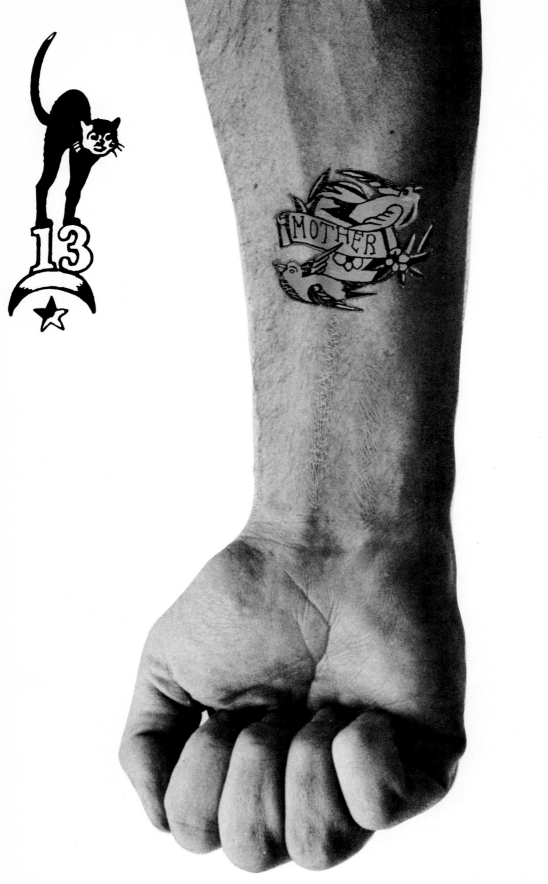

A gallery of the most popular tattoo designs eloquently bespeaks the status of American taste. It would seem that the subjects depicted here have their greatest—and possibly only—appeal to the low-brow. This is not the case, however. The all-time favorite among the tattooed clientele, the inscription to Mother, shows a striking similarity to the motif most popular on greeting cards. Flowers, birds, babies, butterflies, and seminudes appear not only on the arms, backs, and who-knows-where of some twenty million people but also on book covers and posters, in magazine illustrations, television commercials, and other mass communication media reaching just about everybody.

The two greatest influences on the development of the taste of the American people are (1) the sprawling middle class and (2) the willingness of industry to spend money on art.

Artists no longer work for the wealthy. It has become more profitable to work for people with average incomes. Consider this: Families with annual incomes ranging between $5,000 and $25,000 have, when you lump them into a neat spending unit, over 11 times as much money to spend as their cousins with earnings of over $25,000 a year. Why bother with the poor old riches then?

Those in the business of visual persuasion can ill afford to ignore the tastes and whims of the middle-income group. Much of their work must have a "universal appeal." For this reason, most artists find it hard to deviate from the norm, and much of their work follows the expected format. This sad state of affairs is aggravated by the fact that most art in this country is created under the sponsorship of industry. Few businessmen are willing to undertake the risky assignment of changing and refining public taste. The tendency is to encourage creation of art that will please the majority of purchasers. Exactly what it is that pleases the man-on-the-street is of course open to wide (and subjective) interpretation. It can be safely stated that most businessmen tend to underestimate the receptiveness of the so-called "average" man to artistic innovations, while the *avant-garde* artists tend to overestimate it.

It is difficult to appreciate fully the impact industry has had on art. Never in the history of the world have painters and designers had such powerful sponsorship. The medieval church, the kings, and the noblemen were pikers in comparison. Manufacturers spend over a billion dollars annually in sustaining their Bohemian friends. Financially, at least, artists have never had it so good. And because of the availability of funds, America—more than France, Germany, or any other country—has become a mecca for artists. This country has developed commercial art into a big business. It has yet to turn it into a truly artistic one.

The staggering number of paperbacks sold—about a million copies a day—would indicate that the American public is becoming more erudite. Maybe so. Still, the vast majority of cover designs merely display the high points of the story rather than anything even remotely concerned with art. More restrained design (*below*) is slowly coming to fore, but only on books which obviously appeal to the high-brow.

Pansies always stand for
thoughts —
At least that's what folks say.
So this just comes to show
my thoughts
Are there with you today.

Of the some five billion greeting cards sold yearly, the perennial best seller (issued by Joyce Hall) is this 5-cent "Friendship" card. Flowers are as important to the sale of cards as covers displaying seminudes are to paperback books. Hearts, birds, bunnies, cherubs, pussycats, Santas, Easter eggs, one or more babies are familiar themes found at the top of the card list, too. More sophisticated cards (*below*) snatch only a tiny segment of a large market.

On television, performers with more obvious techniques get the highest ratings. Red Skelton has been taking spills in front of the cameras for years and is still going strong. By his own admission, his humor is "easily understandable to the masses because it deals with their own problems." French pantomimist Marcel Marceau played to full houses during his stay in this country, but his subtle comedy is still far from a box-office bonanza.

you...

Be really refreshed! Cool off with Coke! Only Coca-Cola gives you the cheerful lift that's bright and lively... the cold crisp taste that deeply satisfies! No wonder Coke refreshes you best!

FOR THE PAUSE THAT REFRESHES

The American public wants realism in advertising art, too. This is why—and not just for aesthetic reasons—about 80 per cent of all ads feature photography, not drawings or paintings. Everything else being equal, photographic illustrations receive higher readership. When Coca-Cola switched from photography to well-designed drawings, readership dropped. The company reluctantly went back to using photography.

Traditional architecture still dominates the building industry. Over 90 per cent of all houses are built according to the true-and-tried styles of yesterday. This is especially evident in the mass-produced houses in the $15,000 to $30,000 category. Banks are wary of mortgaging homes which can be classified as "off-beat." Modern houses still mark the eccentric or the well-to-do person who has nothing better to do with his money.

Under the sun of the Caribbean, talented Jack Potter pictures a cheerful pause for Coca-Cola.

WHEREVER YOU CRUISE THE CARIBBEAN... when the moment comes for Coca-Cola, here, too, you find it ready for you. In more than 100 countries of the world today, the good taste that distinguishes Coca-Cola makes its enjoyment a happy social custom. Have a Coke, best-loved sparkling drink in all the world.

Coca-Cola   SIGN OF GOOD TASTE

Perhaps no other medium points up the preoccupation of the American public with realistic renderings as much as the twenty-four-sheet posters. Many of the current billboard designs often display a profound ignorance of good graphics, and sometimes of sound advertising. Since the art technique is almost always the same—realistic rendering of a "human interest" situation—the posters appear to have come off the same conveyor belt. The colorful and highly visible poster techniques so popular in Europe have little place in America. Even the slightest deviation from the "norm" causes raised eyebrows (see below) among the advertisers of twenty-four-sheet posters.

Collecting fine *objets d'art* for the purpose of displaying one's wealth—and, more important, one's good taste—became a popular pastime among the well-to-do long before the publication of Vance Packard's *Status Seekers*. Sometimes beauty became synonymous with anything glittering or ornamental, espe-

cially if the object was imported from far-away lands. This living room, thrown together circa 1878, offers a typical example of earnest, if not naive, early American attempts to furnish a room in a "refined" manner.

Merrihome Studio

The average American is unsure of his own taste. He is willing to listen to expert opinion. If this is not forthcoming, he prefers to play it safe and pick what he considers is the "right thing" for him.

The three lamps shown on these pages demonstrate dramatically the shaky confidence American purchasers place in their own artistic judgment. The lamp on the extreme left symbolizes the gingerbread style so popular in the Victorian age but still bought by those who confuse gilding with sound design. Shown on the page is a "modern" lamp. Such monstrosities are very popular among buyers who assume that anything contemporary represents the *avant-garde*. At the center is another type of lamp, an old jug with a handpainted apple design. The lamps on either side outsell this one because buyers—subconsciously—are able to relate themselves to them. Only those with full confidence in their taste dare to go for the handsomest in the lot: the lamp in the center.

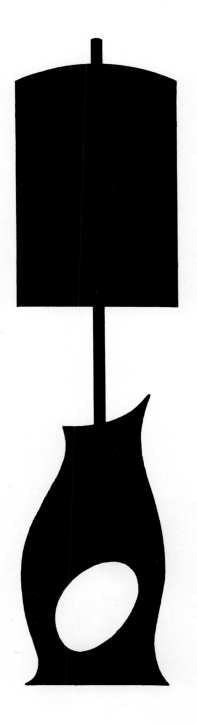

Uncertainty of one's own taste makes car-purchasing habits highly predictable. Cadillac's advertising appeals to middle-brows who would like to be considered high-brows. Jaguar's, on the other hand, appeals to full-blooded high-brows who want to display not their wealth but their intellect. Potential Cadillac purchasers are not particularly attracted to the type of pictures Jaguar uses; neither are Jaguar owners unduly impressed by the splendor of Cadillac's photography. Rarely, if ever, do Jaguar owners switch their loyalties to Cadillacs. They consider themselves a different breed altogether. Jaguars sell best in the New York suburbs and California. Highest saturation of Cadillac owners: Harlem in New York City.

Some things are considered beautiful because of what they *are*. Shown here are such lucky objects: a flower, a fan, a butterfly, and an ornament. The average American feels comfortable discussing their artistic merits; he can voice an opinion that he senses is no longer only his. He can freely assume that anybody in his right mind *knows* that flowers, fans, butterflies, and fancy curlicues are beautiful.

There can be no question about the beauty of a sunset. Even the schmaltziest rendition of this extravaganza (a garish illustration on a post card, for example) will do. In contrast, the classic grace of Venus de Milo befuddles some people; many wonder what happened to the arms of the poor girl.

Based on everything that has been said, the reader may come to the conclusion at this point that the taste of the American public is indeed in bad shape. He may wonder if there is a flicker of hope anywhere on the horizon.

Making long-range predictions is of course not the purpose of this book. Neither is it the intention of your author to complain, criticize, or jump to rash conclusions. Rather, an attempt has been made to report the state of affairs as they are and to let the reader make his own judgment therefrom.

Before final judgment is passed, however, a few factors should be mentioned. One is this: The taste of the public is getting better, not worse.

There are a few very good reasons for making this optimistic statement. Let us look at some other factors:

Americans have innate curiosity about their surroundings. They want to learn.

This country is going through a cultural revolution at a tempo never before experienced in history. It took the Greeks, Romans, English, and French several centuries to establish a culture they could call their own. Neither was the Renaissance an abrupt awakening from the slumber of the Middle Ages; rather, it was a slow, tedious —and subtle—intellectual evolution lasting four or five hundred years.

Compare this to the rate at which things are moving in this country. In less than a hundred years Americans have grown from complete cultural boors to the largest group of art purchasers in the world.

Culture is being devoured in this country at incredible speed. Twenty-four of the largest museums have shown a jump of 28 per cent in attendance during the last two years, and they were doing fine before that. More people attend museums than baseball games. There are some 4,500 art galleries in this country, more than anywhere else in the world. And Americans are not only looking at art; they are buying it in increasing quantities as well, from the three million Utrillo prints (98 cents and up) to the $871,850 paid out for "originals" at a single benefit auction not so long ago.

Apparently an increasing number of people, young and old, are making an effort to find out about the finer things in life. Today it is possible to put on good shows on television and get a fair share of the audience; in New York City 30,000 letters of protest poured in when the cancellation of a series of plays, produced by a local station, was announced. The number of "art" movie houses has jumped from 12 to 550 in the last fifteen years. And surprisingly enough, it has also become feasible to publish "good" paperback books. Sales figures for such classics as the *Iliad* and the *Odyssey* long ago passed the half-million mark. And what really amazed the cynics was the success of the "hardcover" monthly magazine, *Horizon*, ·which carries no advertising but has plenty of handsomely reproduced four-color illustrations of the works of artists, living and dead. "This magazine," explained Editorial Director Joseph J. Thorndike, Jr., "is edited for intelligent, college-educated people . . . not the all-day watcher of television, or those whose aspirations begin, or end, with the solid gold Cadillac." The magazine went into the black almost immediately.

Like a child shown a picture book for the first time, Americans are almost pathetically eager to find out about art. Equipped with an outsized inferiority complex about their alleged cultural shortcomings, they turn to night schools, libraries, lectures, and friends for advice. Magazines that make it their policy to improve people's tastes are being rewarded with a substantial rise in circulation figures. Within ten years *Vogue* managed to increase its sale of copies 78 per cent, *House Beautiful*, 88 per cent. Interior decorators are busier than ever; the two major national professional organizations (National Society of Interior Designers and American Institute of Decorators) report a more than threefold increase in their membership in less than half a decade. Not only do individuals hire experts for counsel, but so do large companies. It seems that almost everyone wants to find out just what is meant by "good taste."

Americans are getting more education. They are getting it more ways than one.

An increasing number of people graduate from

college and live happily ever after. The 1959 enrollment in colleges and universities totaled almost 3½ million, meaning that for eight consecutive years new records have been set. Just before World War II, only about 15 per cent of those between 18 and 21 years old had gone beyond high school; now, almost 40 per cent continue on to college.

But it's not only a formal education that makes Americans more receptive to culture. With more education comes a more expansive curiosity that lasts for a lifetime. Americans travel more than ever before (and have more money to enjoy their journeys), visit more places, not only *looking* harder at their surroundings but also *seeing* more.

And yet, Americans have a long way to go. They may know what is good and what is not, but not why. Intellectual understanding of art is being confused with emotional understanding.

The race for culture is on—Americans merrily flounder in it—and yet something seems to be missing. With all the time and money spent on enjoyment of "culture," why do our neighbors, near and far (and sometimes even our own social critics), still so often consider us insensitive louts? Why should we be put upon to live down the stereotyped image of the American tourist making the rounds of galleries in European cities, wearing a checkered sport shirt, a Sunday camera slung over his shoulder, and chewing a stick of gum?

Unfortunately old traditions still linger on, and they do slow down progress. In the first place, we are in too much of a hurry to become cultured. The whole affair has turned into a national pastime, an assignment with a deadline, like sending missiles to the moon. And in our giddy rush to become a nation of gently bred ladies and gentlemen, we have overlooked one of the most important ingredients in becoming cultured: tranquility. It is difficult to enjoy art in a frenzied state of mind.

We tend to look for the "facts" about a painting rather than the inherent qualities that make it a timeless masterpiece; preoccupation with facts, too, is part of our culture. More people than ever before take courses in art appreciation, follow charming hostesses on guided tours of museums, go sight-seeing to Europe. Everyone wants to learn fast and become knowledgeable about art in six easy lessons. But what we would mostly like to find out consists of "essential information," the name and dates of the artist and the number of illegitimate children he sired during his lifetime. An earnest desire to develop his artistic taste notwithstanding, the average American is still more intrigued by Van Gogh's right ear than the artist's swirling, restless painting style.

And yet the public's taste is steadily improving. Prosperity allows us to turn toward the enjoyment of art. To be artistically sensitive is becoming less and less a privilege of eccentrics only. The future holds out significant promise. And—fortunately or unfortunately—there is but one way we *can* go. Up.

2

The changing face of models

1900

Americans' favorite in that period was the aristocratic, evasive Gibson girl—the dame with the enigmatic smile.

1961   The most consistently successful box-office heroine today is blonde, freckle-faced Doris Day—the gal with the friendly laugh.

The "girl next door" came into her own. Today, she is no longer the exclusive property of the poor; she is everybody's pal. She is a persuasive sales girl.

There is overwhelming evidence that girls with a glint in their eyes do a better selling job than their more aloof sisters. This doesn't mean that all models in today's advertisements must appear in blue jeans and a soggy pair of sneakers. Like Doris Day in the movies, they can appear in gowns specially designed for them by the fashion houses of Paris, in jewelry that would be better kept in safes, in hairdos that add another 10 inches to their height. They can wrap themselves in almost anything as long as they manage to convey some sense of warmth, good sportsmanship, and social accessibility.

During the early stage of advertising, women acted a bit more ladylike; usually they just stood still, giving the reader the benefit of their presence and very little else. Occasionally, they permitted a faint smile to appear on their lips, and once in a great while they could be seen on the arm of a gentleman whose primary function was to throw admiring glances at his companion. Rarely did these damsels indulge in the act of running, jumping, or climbing trees—occurrences that are far from rare in today's advertising and editorial photographs.

Why the change? Modern girls are not what their grandmas used to be. Almost as many coeds as men go to college, and that's just the beginning. They work and make money. Even more important, women's ideas of themselves have changed. Most wives consider themselves more or less on equal footing with their husbands.

The girl with the perfect face, the well-polished feminine manners, is losing some of her popularity. Hectic suburban living, which calls for wives who can take the good with the bad, has increased the need for women who can make quick adjustments. Hence the growing importance of the "corporation wife," who can talk shop with her husband's boss over a dinner put together at last-minute notice. These are all important considerations influencing modern man's choice of his squaw.

Research studies indicate that pictures of aloof beauties have good attention-getting value but often disappointingly little impact on readership. Apparently readers stop and admire the transcendence of the model—as one would a marble statue of Aphrodite—but are afraid to become emotionally involved with her.

Of course a friendly smile, or any other sign of life, might quickly change the reader's opinion of her.

Women are more willing than men to accept overly glamorous vixens—as long as they act as symbols of women, not as real people. Thus in fashion photographs it is perfectly acceptable for the model to wear a disdainful smile along with the latest in women's hats; her role in the picture is that of a mannequin. In cosmetics, too, it is permissible for the model to perform in an icy manner since obviously the whole thing is only an act to get her man.

What kind of girl is America's darling?

Perhaps the most convincing demonstrations of changing public taste in beautiful women happen at the national beauty queen elections held in Atlantic City. No longer is it sufficient for a candidate to be the proud possessor of certain body measurements; she must also prove to her public that she can talk. The winner is then judged not only on the basis of her looks but on her performance as a reciter of poems, singer of ballads, dancer of minuets, and cook of cherry pies as well. The beauty queen, more often than not, has a remarkable resemblance to the American public's image of the "girl next door."

Sought-after professional models are able to display a wide gamut of emotions. They establish quick—and profound—contact with their audience.

With the declining demand for frozen-faced maidens, the girl with the flexible personality has come to the fore. Professional models today, just as successful movie actresses, must be able to convey feeling to their onlookers. A pretty smile no longer suffices in itself; now it must *look* convincing. Successful models have this talent. Dolores Hawkins (whose interpretations of a smile are on the right-hand page), Suzy Parker and Millie Perkins (two girls whose emoting ability brought them major roles in the movies), and television personalities Julia Meade, Arlene Grey, Jean Sullivan, Patricia Bright, and Betty Furness (all with stage experience) have the ability to convey emotions, real or imaginary. Many models have aspirations of appearing in television plays or Broadway shows and combining their modeling work with a stage career.

Acting ability enables models to switch roles freely. The "mother" hugging an infant and smiling at her husband often is the very same girl whose picture appears on the pages of high-fashion magazines. Conversely, a model labeled "housewife" not infrequently works her way into cosmetic and fashion ads.

Ability to "move" unselfconsciously in front of the camera has become an important qualification to modeling success.

Stiff poses make readers aware of the fact that they are looking at a preplanned picture. Models with agile limbs are gaining increasing popularity with photographers. Many of them attend dance schools in their spare time, ride horseback, go skiing, or indulge in yoga exercises.

Photographers, too, help the "natural look" along with improved shooting techniques. Speed of films has increased significantly in recent years. Manufacturers are steadily refining their stroboscopic equipment. High-speed cameras allow photographers to shoot as many as 20 pictures a second. And it is becoming increasingly practical to go outdoors to get pictures.

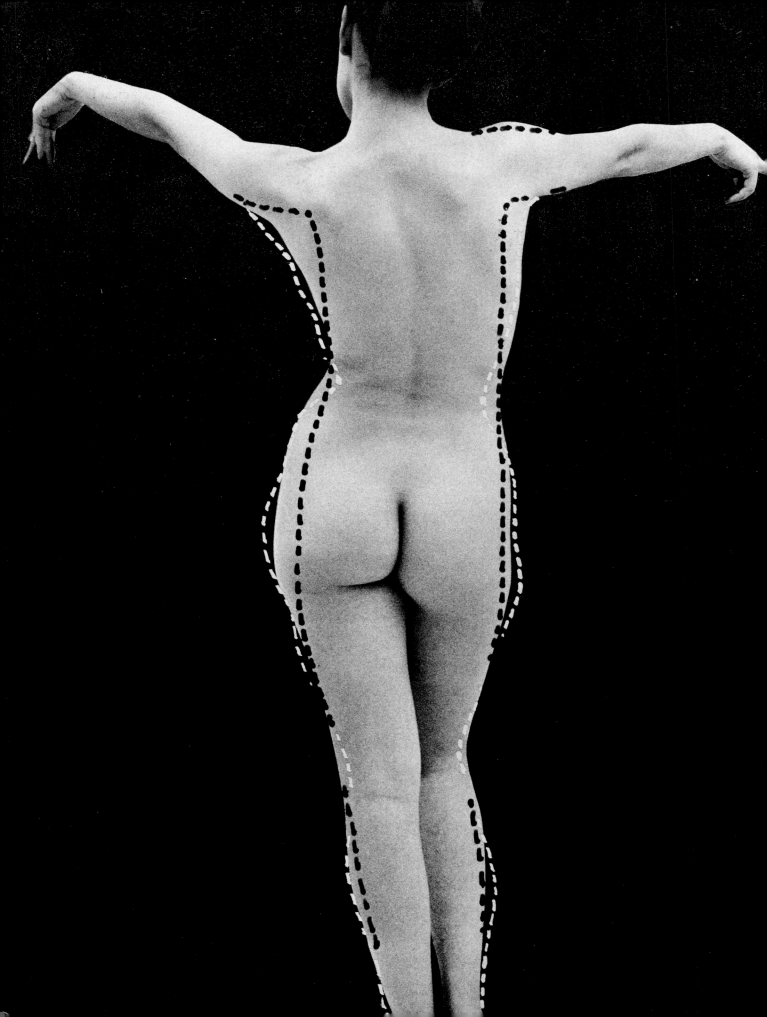

Not only her face but the figure of the ideal woman has changed, too. Three centuries ago, as this painting by Rubens shows, nymphs of generous proportions were the objects of men's affections. Glamour in those days was synonymous with earthy, rotund femininity.

In the roaring twenties, the ladies shed considerable weight. Enjoying their newly discovered freedom, girls went all out to demonstrate equality of the sexes. Tubular figures like the one shown here were in vogue.

Today's woman has put back some flesh in the right places. It is doubtful whether the robust maiden of medieval times will ever stage a comeback. Most photographer's models are usually on and off various diets. Says the head of a successful modeling agency: "I turn down half of all applicants for the same reason: too much weight in the rump." Even the tallest of girls is expected to have a waist 11 inches slimmer than her hips and bust. It seems as if the ideal modern woman must combine the qualifications of Rubens' buxom models with those of the flappers of the twenties.

Typical of the girl everybody loves: the "Rheingold Girl"

Every year, through America's "second largest election," the people choose a gal who embodies a peculiar American daydream. She is the girl whom every boy wishes to marry and every man wishes he had.

The Rheingold Girl is not a complicated person. Judging from the photographs in which she appears, she spends little—if any—of her spare time reading, solving crossword puzzles, rooting for important national issues, visiting galleries, or designing a new type submarine. Her problems, one feels, are simple, such as what sandals to wear with which bathing suit.

All her public asks her to do is to be a human being—and this alone represents an accomplishment for a girl as pretty as she. Miss Rheingold can be found at beaches, ski resorts, yacht clubs, golf courses, tennis courts, picnics, and any other place that promises fun. What makes her so likable is this: She fits into any kind of situation. She skis, swims, rides horseback, plays tennis or golf with skill, almost (but not quite) as well as the boys with whom she surrounds herself. She may not be able to whip up a rock lobster casserole with mushrooms at a moment's notice, but she is good at hamburgers. She drives a car and helps the boys wash theirs. She adores sitting around fireplaces and singing. About her only vice is her predilection for beer. But, under the circumstances, this is forgivable.

The Rheingold Girl likes everyone and is liked by everyone.

Perhaps more than anything else in her favor is the Rheingold Girl's ability to get along with people. She not only makes a hit with the younger generation; her charm also beguiles older men less romantically inclined. Her sweet disposition makes women accept her, too.

Miss Rheingold—the girl who is "one of the boys"—is a symbol of today's heroine. Her demeanor is a far cry from the sultry aloofness of yesterday's girl whose favorite spot was her place on top of the pedestal.

Interestingly, both blondes and brunettes have developed an image of themselves. Blondes are associated with two well-defined prototypes. There is the "dumb blonde," beautiful, baby-faced, bedecked with jewelry and a fur coat. Her specialty is sex. Then there is the wholesome freckle-faced blonde who typifies the "girl next door." She is the marrying type. Almost always she is an "outdoor girl".

Dark-haired girls have a more subtle kind of sex appeal based on their alleged seductiveness. This type is often found indoors. Brunettes—in the minds of the public—are apt to talk slower. be taller, and have less need of protection than blondes. Her type is more apt to be associated with "class." Pictures of brunettes get more attention from women than those of blondes.

1920 ∽ 1921 ∽ 1922 ∽ 1923 ∽ 1924 ∽ 1925 ∽ 1926 ∽ 1927 ∽ 1928 ∽ 1929 ∽ 1930 ∽ 1931 ∽ 193

1951 ∽ 1952 ∽ 1953 ∽ 1954 ∽ 1955 ∽ 1956 ∽ 1957 ∽ 1958 ∽ 1959 ∽ 1960 ∽ 1961 ∽ 1962 ∽ 196

Today male idols are not necessarily the best-looking. A handsome face is no longer synonymous with the classic profile; men with broken noses, wrinkled foreheads, crooked mouths, eye patches, and even bald heads are considered attractive.

It is doubtful whether Rudolph Valentino and the good-looking young man in the Arrow Shirt advertisements could sustain the kind of success they had in their day. Both the American male and female opinions on what constitutes good-looking men have changed radically.

Prettiness in man is considered uninteresting. And worse still, in most people's minds, consciously or unconsciously, this quality is labeled as being not too masculine. Depth interviewing reveals that women long for strong, masculine leadership in their lives and that (not always justifiably) they tend to confuse prettiness with softness. Unless she is the kind who likes to play the role of a mother to her husband (as the female admirers of Liberace), the average woman shows preference for a man who handles himself well in the vicissitudes of life and who has a few wrinkles (or eye patches) to prove it.

Consider today's top movie idols. Some are very handsome, but even the best-looking aren't "pretty." Cary Grant, Gregory Peck, Yul Brynner, and John Wayne are all men of impressive appearance, but their faces (and personalities) suggest that they have led full and colorful lives, not completely free of crisis. Some of the most popular movie actors go even a step further; they look for problems (and usually find them) so that they can suffer to their hearts' content. Marlon Brando is famous for his emotional struggles, and so is Anthony Perkins. James Dean's claim to fame was his ability to symbolize all the difficulties youth had ever faced. This made him a man of considerable stature.

Some successful movie actors are not even handsome, at least not in the traditional sense. Any second-rate baseball team can come up with more acceptable-looking specimens than James Cagney, Fred Astaire, Broderick Crawford. Yet these men are thrust into romantic roles and usually come out as the winners. Apparently looks aren't everything.

In today's advertisements it is possible to couple young girls with men ten, fifteen, and sometimes even twenty years their senior.

A man doesn't even have to be young any more to make girls sigh. Clark Gable was still playing romantic roles in his sixties. Gary Cooper was out to get Audrey Hepburn, almost forty years his junior, in one of his movies, and he accomplished his mission without undue difficulty. When *McCall's* magazine asked an all-girl jury to pick the two dozen "most attractive men in the world," not one of the lucky winners turned out to be less than thirty years old; over half were in their fifties, and two of them (Dr. Albert Schweitzer and Bernard Baruch) had passed eighty.

In advertising the trend toward older men is noticeable. For years, a slightly bald gentleman was depicted with a girl young enough to be his mistress in the highly successful British Woollen series. Commander Whitehead is old enough to have his beard grown fifty times over, yet the admiring glances of the ladies in the Schweppes ads seem to prove the old Briton is doing all right. So are all the Marlboro characters, from the ages of twenty-five to fifty-five.

The search for "interesting" men goes on.

Curiously enough, a great many men appearing in today's advertisements are not professional models at all. More than anyone else, they themselves are astonished that someone would want to photograph them for publication.

Photographers and art directors are on a never-ending lookout for new "talent," i.e., interesting faces. Male model agencies and actors' guilds always have a few personalities on hand, but the demand exceeds the supply. More often than not, an office building, the house next door, a gym, or the Bowery offers as good a source as any. Some photographers have files on people found in these various places and keep close track of them all. And the search is ever-continuing. As American women change their outlook, the change is reflected in the faces of American men in mass-communication media.

Models who do not look the part are becoming increasingly popular with photographers. They help make the ads more unusual. They also tend to establish quick identification with their audiences who "recognize" characters they "know." Most people here are not professional models; many were posing for the first time in their lives.

Women who are not "ideal beauties" appear with increasing frequency in today's communication media.

Girls wearing eyeglasses are no longer automatically put in the category of hopeless spinsters; the model shown here appeared in an advertisement *not* as an old-maid schoolteacher. The gal (on the right) looking up at her man with a telling glance fails to meet the circumscribed measurements of a "beautiful girl" (she is slightly over five feet tall), yet her appearance in the Pacific Sheet advertisement helped to make the photograph a resounding success. French actress Simone Signoret received critical accolade and box-office success in America when she demonstrated that sex appeal is not the exclusive property of the very young. The American public is revising (and broadening) its stereotyped concept of "beauty."

3

For the subconscious only

Seeing is a state of mind.

"Seeing" is more than the mechanical process of receiving messages. With the recognition of an object goes a variety of responses. Sometimes they are wholly automatic, as in the case of a fish; sometimes they involve a chain of bodily responses, as proved in the experiments of scientist Ivan Petrovich Pavlov; and sometimes they produce a vastly complex series of emotions, as is true with humans.

In the art of visual persuasion, the understanding of associations that every picture, without exception, brings forth is essential.

To an advertiser, or any other kind of visual communicator, the illustration per se has little value. What he is interested in is the *effect* of the picture, which may be something totally different from one's logical assumption.

It is unfortunate—and often the cause of a waste of vast sums of money—that in trying to evaluate pictures (be they paintings or corporate symbols) the critics tend to underestimate the significance of subtleties that create associations. Businessmen usually judge the effectiveness of visual devices on a purely rational basis, forgetting that people react to images as automatically (and unanalytically) as a small child to a piece of candy. Of course, it is easier to pass judgment on the more obvious, explainable aspects of an illustration (perspective, accuracy in rendering) than on such intangible factors as "mood," psychological effect of colors, and the implication of deliberate distortions. Appreciation of these latent qualities in a picture requires not only high intelligence but also sensitive artistic intuition.

To demonstrate the importance of association, the lines on these two pages assume a "personality" of their own. As the position of the lines changes so do our reactions to them.

More examples of subtleties that give pictures unexpected power will be shown throughout this chapter.

This horizontal line, reposing quietly on imaginary ground, evokes feelings of tranquility in the beholder.

The same line, now turned on end to a vertical position, suggests impending activity. The line appears to have aspirations of its own, radiating confidence, even pride.

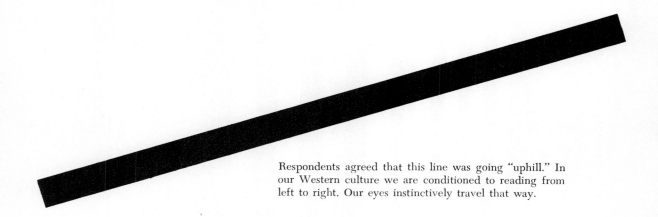

When a group of 50 people were asked which side represented the "end" of this line, they all pointed to the right.

Respondents agreed that this line was going "uphill." In our Western culture we are conditioned to reading from left to right. Our eyes instinctively travel that way.

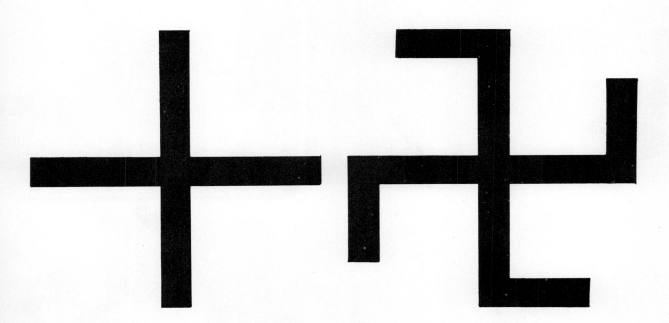

Symbols are created through a process of association. The cross has been the symbol of high purpose through the ages. It helps in reflecting the image of such meritorious organizations as the Red Cross.

Associations change with the times. The swastika is one of the most ancient and widespread of all ornamental forms. It generally stood for well-being and good luck. The activities of Adolf Hitler have altered this image.

Packages can have a "sex" of their own, depending on such subtle factors as texture and design. Here, package innovator Michael Mura successfully manipulated the gender of six cubes all the same size. The three above connote masculinity; bold stripes, a piece of rope, and a wooden surface are all symbols of men.

The three cubes shown in this photograph take on more gentle, feminine personalities. They would be more at home on cosmetic or fashion counters. Soft fur, pattern of thin stripes, and velvet ribbon all belong to the world of women. Such colors as white, pink, and other pastel shades would make these boxes appear even more "feminine."

Shapes, too, have definite sexual implications. As a rule, round objects seem more "feminine" while angular articles suggest "masculinity."

This psychological principle has important commercial applications. A manufacturer must, during the early stages of merchandising, decide upon the "sex" of the package in which his product will be put. Should a man's hat be packed in a round box, for example? (A hexagonal shape is more acceptable.) Should a woman's toilet soap be oval or square? (Oval is more desirable.) Should detergents be packaged in square boxes? (Yes. Detergents have been found to move faster if they connote masculinity—power and action-mindedness—even though buyers are mainly women.)

Almost every object has a "sex" of its own. This fact is important to keep in mind when choosing symbols or props for an illustration.

The rough texture of a potato helps make it a masculine article. A tomato, soft and pretty, has become a symbol of femininity. An apple has no sex (it grows on "masculine" trees, but in the Bible it served as a symbol of feminine beguilement).

Trees (and wooden textures) reek of masculinity. Delicacy of flowers (and girls' liking for them) assures their place in a woman's domain. Grass, on the other hand, has no claim to any particular gender.

Black has strength opacity. These qual make it appear more m culine than feminine. translucency of w (and its virginal qual gives it a maidenly pearance. Gray is in tween and therefore m ter.

MASCULINE

POTATO

TREE

BLACK

FEMININE

TOMATO

FLOWER

WHITE

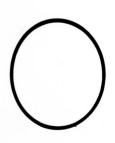

NEUTER

APPLE

GRASS

GRAY

...in is a "he." It sug-
... power, adventure,
...y. A ship, by virtue
... sleek, graceful ap-
...nce, has managed to
...ne a "she." The car
...to be more masculine
... feminine, but in this
...rn world it is rapidly
...ning bisexual.

Wool (tweedy textures) is associated more with men's suits than ladies' dresses. Silk has a different connotation altogether; its softness and pliability make it more "feminine." Cotton can be either gender.

A dog is usually "he." A cat—characteristically calculating animal—is "she." Both looks and personalities give these creatures a "sex" of their own. A horse can be "he" or "she," depending on the anatomy.

The harsh, angular edges of square objects (as shown on previous page) suggest masculine temper while the round shape of a circle implies the gentleness of a woman. A triangle stands undecided.

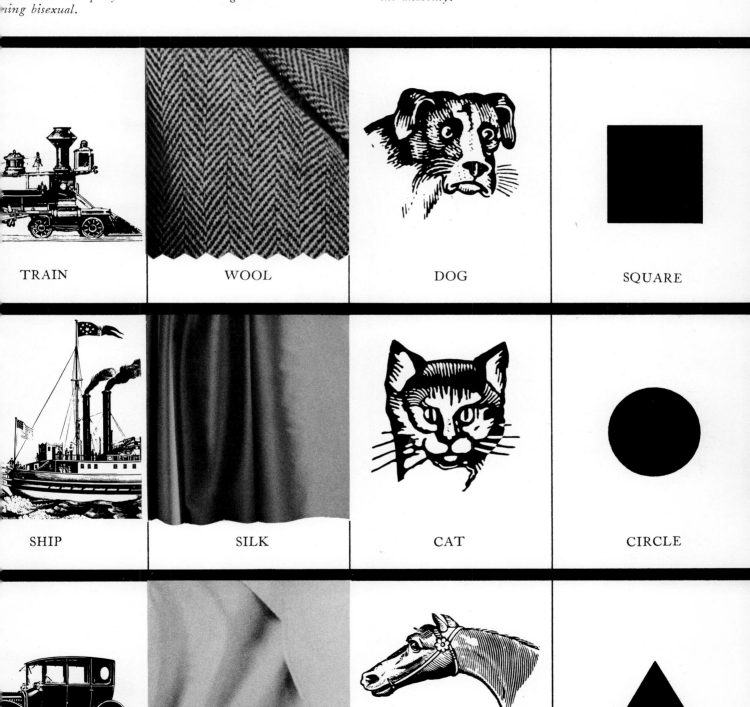

TRAIN WOOL DOG SQUARE

SHIP SILK CAT CIRCLE

...UTOMOBILE LINEN HORSE TRIANGLE

An interesting example here shows how the sex of a "neuter" (an automobile in this case) can be manipulated. The picture of an automobile shown above has strong masculine connotations even though a driver is not visible. The vehicle is moving across rough terrain, is dominating its environment; it suggests (like the car going uphill) a forceful, *active* personality.

The automobile in this instance is presented in a more tranquil environment. It is standing still. Both doors are open, implying that two passengers—presumably a man and a woman—have gone for a walk; this possibility suggests romance. Here the automobile (like the one going downhill) assumes a more quiet, *passive* disposition.

"Sex" of a television show can also be decided in advance. Above is a sequence from the title section of a series based on cases from Scotland Yard. The man's entanglement with law and order is symbolically dramatized by the crossbars jumping quickly and unexpectedly into the picture, closing out the lonely figure's only avenue to freedom. Angular two-dimensional design and the presence of only a male performer create a masculine atmosphere.

On the other hand, a commercial for Modess (on the right-hand page) is feminine in feeling. The appearance of round dots (accompanied by soft Debussy-style music) gradually fusing into a picture of a beautiful girl appeals to the aesthetic sensibilities of women.

Optical illusions occur because of fixed ideas. On top: the taller container appears to hold more. Height is often associated with volume. The dot in the right corner of this page seems larger than its true size; our eyes are unaccustomed to seeing an oversized dot. Even more gigantic seems the chicken on the opposite page, though it measures less than one-fifth the actual size of a live fowl; it is its relationship to the page which makes it appear so large.

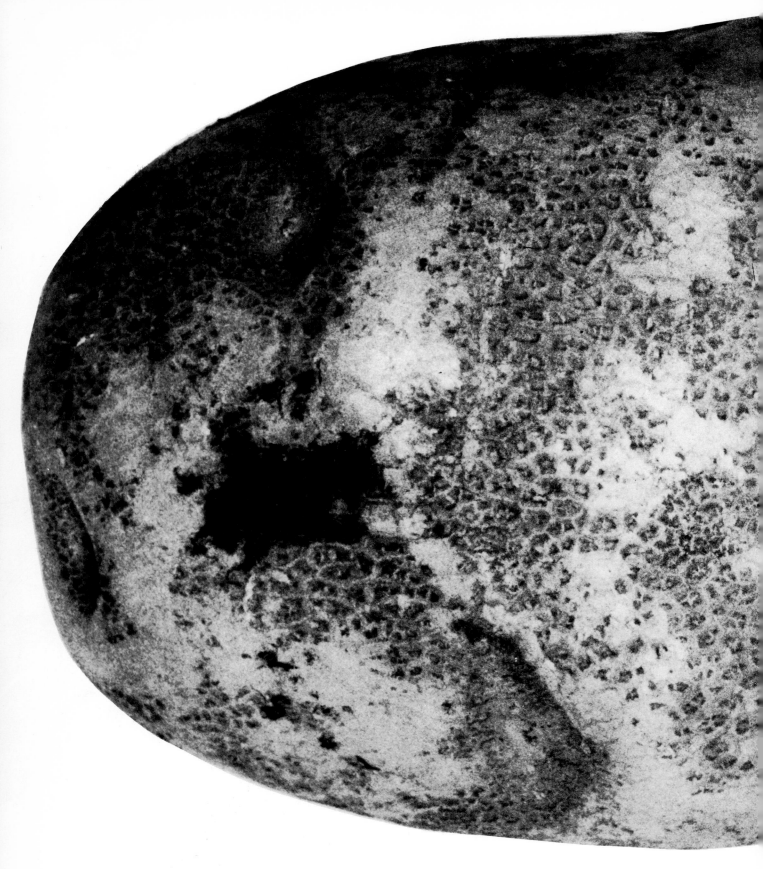

Some objects, like the potato above, cannot be blown up indiscriminately and still retain their identity. Our eyes are not conditioned to accepting giant potatoes; this represents a totally new optical experience.

Equally difficult is the recognition of this gentleman as seen from a straight-down view. Rarely do we see people from such an acute angle. Thus we do not recognize the image—even though it is a realistic photograph.

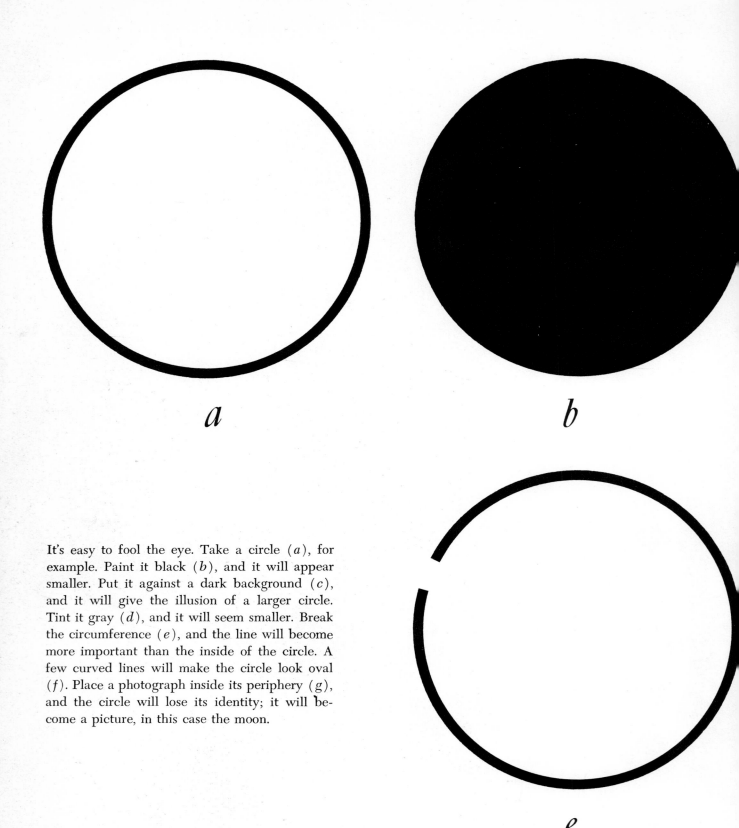

a

b

It's easy to fool the eye. Take a circle (*a*), for example. Paint it black (*b*), and it will appear smaller. Put it against a dark background (*c*), and it will give the illusion of a larger circle. Tint it gray (*d*), and it will seem smaller. Break the circumference (*e*), and the line will become more important than the inside of the circle. A few curved lines will make the circle look oval (*f*). Place a photograph inside its periphery (*g*), and the circle will lose its identity; it will become a picture, in this case the moon.

e

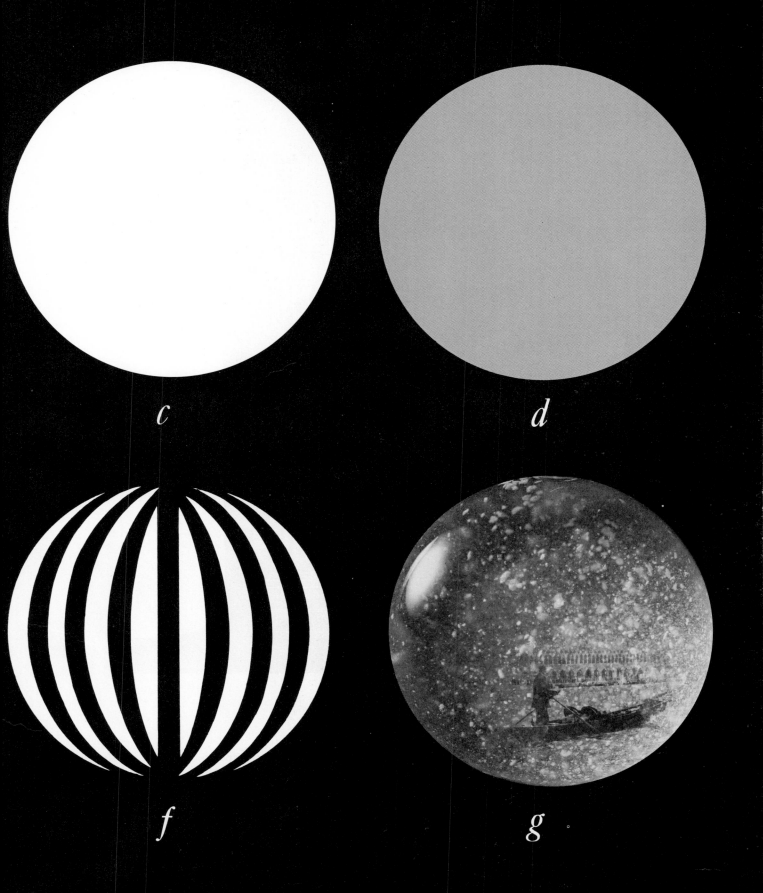

c

d

f

g

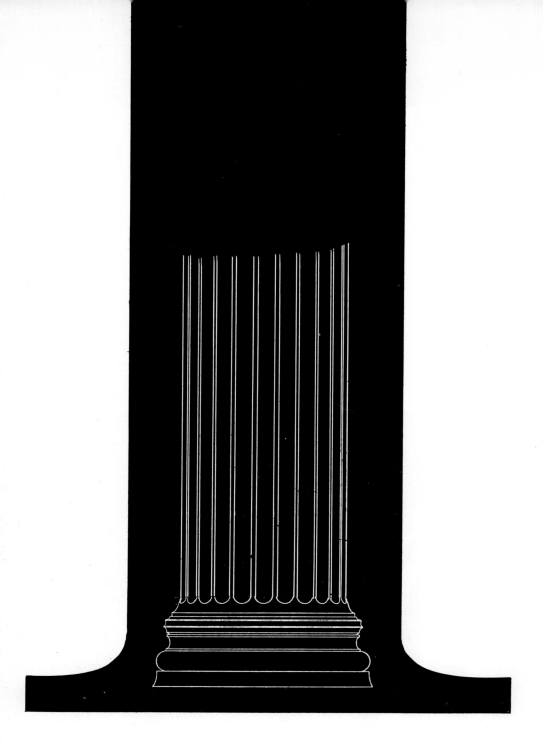

Type faces, too, have personalities all their own. The "feel" of type depends on its structure: the relationship of thick and thin lines, the rounded or squared-off quality of corners. Based on these factors type faces assume a personality, as for example, the Caslon letter, which is derived from the classic architecture of ancient Greece:

abcdefghijklmnopqrstuvwxyzabcdefghijklmnopqrstuvwx

A survey conducted for *Advertising Requirements* revealed some interesting reactions that people had to type faces. Two groups were questioned: experts and laymen. The results are shown on the right-hand page (line 1 set in this type face indicates adjectives used by experts; line 2 set in this type face shows reactions of laymen alone; line 3 set in this type face describes the feelings of both groups).

Bodoni Book

Light, rich, beautiful, expensive, meaningful, graceful, tight, formal
Soft
Perfect, good, clean, harmonious, honest

Bodoni Book Italic

Perfect
Soft, plain, feminine
Good, rich, beautiful, rounded, expensive, graceful, clean, harmonious

Bodoni, Ultra

Active
Ugly
Hard, strong, dark, masculine, rugged

Cheltenham Bold

Imperfect, hard, constrained, old, ugly, old-fashioned, cheap
Active, honest
Plain, strong, dark, simple, masculine, usual, rugged

Tempo Bold

New, modern
Hard, plain, good, strong dark, simple, masculine, rugged, honest

Karnak Intermediate

1. Hard, constrained, strong, masculine, rugged, awkward, stiff
2. Good, simple, clean, honest

Kaufman Script

1. *New, active, modern, informal*
2. *Soft, feminine*
3. *Light, delicate*

Typo Script

1. *Old-fashioned*
2. *Weak, beautiful*
3. *Soft, ornate, light complex, rich, rounded, expensive, feminine, delicate, graceful, clean, harmonious, formal*

Garamond

1. Light, rich, beautiful, rounded, expensive, meaningful, delicate, graceful, formal
2. Plain
3. Perfect, good, clean, harmonious, honest

Garamond Bold

1. **Old, meaningful**
2. **Hard, plain, usual, rugged**
3. **Perfect, strong, dark, masculine, clean, harmonious, honest**

Garamond Italic

1. *Perfect, good, rich, beautiful, rounded, meaningful, harmonious, honest*
2. *Ornate, weak*
3. *Soft, light, expensive, feminine, delicate, graceful, clean*

Flash

1. *Free, new, active, strong, rounded, modern, cheap, masculine, relaxed*
2. *Dark, rugged, informal*

love
---
home
---
war
---
child
---
mother
---
night
---
laughter

Certain words, like the ones shown here, evoke powerful picture associations. In this case, the type face in which the word is set becomes less important. The meaning of the message overshadows the graphics. Yet even this kind of "pure" word communication can hardly be called verbal. The words here evoke vivid visual images—as we can readily find out by shutting our eyes and letting our minds roam freely. As a matter of fact, the reader makes up his own world of pictures as soon as his eyes hit the page; hence the emotional impact of these words.

Shown on the right-hand page is an example of how a single word combined with a picture can sometimes take the place of a long complicated headline—and still tell a powerful story.

love

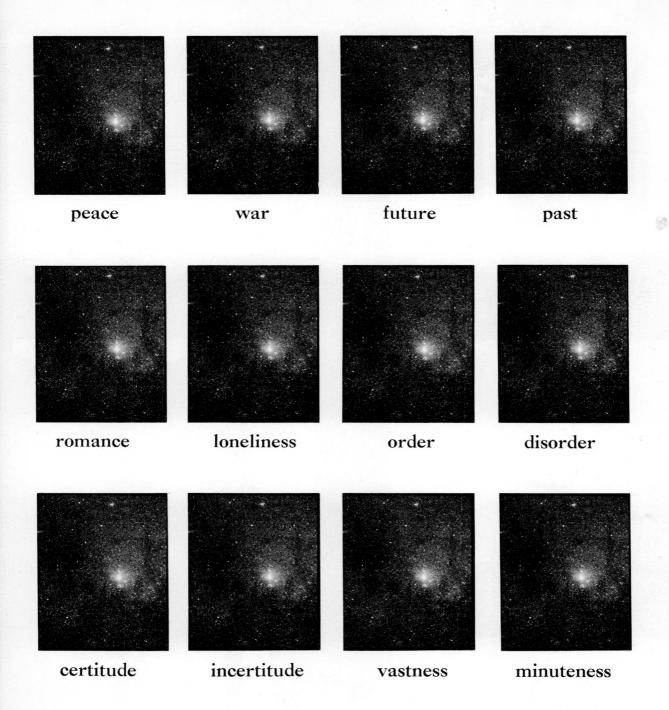

peace   war   future   past

romance   loneliness   order   disorder

certitude   incertitude   vastness   minuteness

Just as words evoke picture images, so pictures bring up word associations. The same picture can have many meanings depending on the context in which it appears. In advertising the interplay between words and pictures usually produces a single impression. This is why the illustration and the headline in an ad (or the video and the audio on the television screen) should always be studied as an entity.

**WATCH
OUT**

squirrels

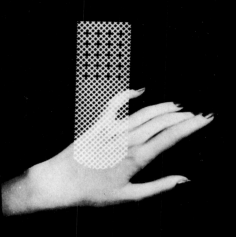

FACE

n●se

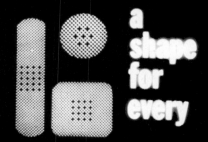

a shape for every

Picture and word symbols are sometimes the easiest—and quickest—means of telling a story. This TV commercial for Johnson & Johnson's Band-Aid dramatically conveys sources of minor injuries. Fast pace, staccato-like presentation, reminds the viewer of how accidents can occur suddenly and unexpectedly.

One of the most important rules in visual persuasion: the public tends to receive a *total* image of an advertisement.

Those responsible for advertising often forget that consumers do not study each element of an advertisement (be it in print or on television) with the same painstaking care as do those who make an ad. The consumer does not analyze. He (or she) *feels.*

Seeing an advertisement for the first time is much like meeting a person. We may not "see" the color of his eyes, the pattern of his necktie, the kind of shoes he is wearing, but we do receive a strong, distinctive impression of his *total* personality. In the same manner all the various elements of an ad (illustration, text, type faces, signature, colors, and layout) work together in making a total impression.

Two advertisements are shown on the right-hand page. The Tussy ad has a "cheerful" look. The Listerine ad is more "somber" in quality. It is not the illustration alone that gives each an individual personality. Every element "fits" into a single, aggregate image.

It is not only the interplay of parts that gives an ad distinction. The environment in which it appears also has an important effect on the image it creates.

An advertisement appearing in a fashion magazine such as *Vogue* may strike the reader differently from one on the pages of *The Saturday Evening Post.*

This consideration becomes especially important in choosing time slots for television commercials. Almost all television shows have "moods" of their own. Cops-and-robbers stories connote violence. Family situations have warmth. Westerns suggest adventure. Kids' shows are uncomplicated. Comedy routines demand something humorous. A commercial that would be right at home in the framework of one show might be jarring in the context of another.

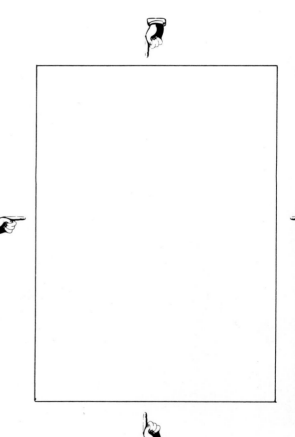

a

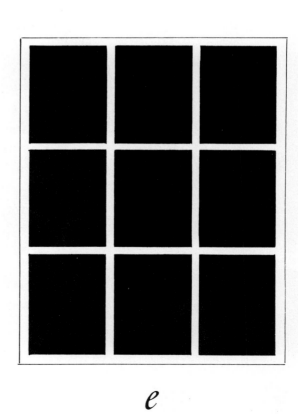

b

d

e

c

f

Everything else being equal, the composition of an advertisement—arrangement of elements on a page—is important in attracting readers.

The content of an advertisement is by far the most important single factor in making it effective. Execution of the art work comes a close second. A third still significant factor is the layout itself.

Here are some interesting findings:

(*a*) A single dominant illustration on top of a page gets a high "noted" rating for the ad. Putting the text above the picture may make the ad "different" but not necessarily increase its readership (there are many exceptions, of course). Mill Shepard found in his study of the 36 best-read ads featured in 12 magazines that only *one* among them did not follow the horizontal picture format.

(*b*) Vertical split (picture on one side, text on the other) discourages some readers. Conditioning plays an important part in this response. We are *accustomed* to seeing pictures *over* text. When photographs of girls lathering their faces were used vertically on the left side of the page, the advertisers of Dove soap saw almost a 50 per cent drop in readership.

(*c*) Bleed pictures, little or no text, usually get high noting and readership. The size of the picture makes an impact and so does unusual format.

(*d*) When scattered on the page, pictures tend to play havoc with readership figures. Lincoln National Life Insurance Company boosted readership of their ads fivefold by combining three pictures into one.

(*e*) Pictures of equal size, arranged regularly on a page, sometimes produce commendable readership. The reader accepts this format as a "single-picture" ad.

(*f*) Close-up of face (or object) gives optical illusion of larger picture. Both noting and reading usually go up.

If there is any one conclusion to be drawn from these findings, it is this: readers do not want to make an effort to decipher ads. *Simplicity pays off*.

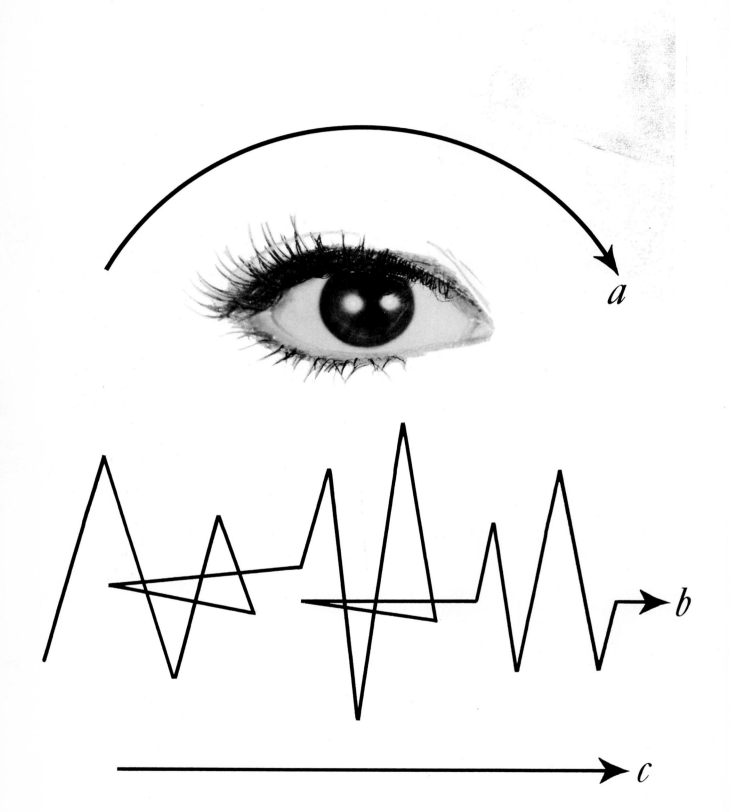

Eye movements are based on conditioned reflexes.

Left-to-right reading habit makes our eyes travel clockwise in exploring an advertisement. The optical center (a) of a page, too, is slightly to the left. Once the exploratory trip is over, there is no telling what the eye will do. More likely than not, it will jump back and forth over the page with incredible speed (b). Overoptimistic indeed is the advertiser who hopes that his readers will scan his layout in an orderly fashion, starting with the picture and finishing with the signature at the bottom of the page.

About the only generalizations that can be made about ocular tendencies are these: The eye prefers to move horizontally (c). Vertical movements are tiring. Clear vision takes place only when the eye is fixed; it is temporarily blinded when in motion (look in the mirror and see if you can detect your eyes moving). We can scan about 1.25 words per fixation. But exceptionally fast readers (over 500 words a minute) are capable of taking in five or six words per fixation.

The movement of eyes reveals much about our subconscious tendencies when looking at a picture. Ocular photography shows that viewers see more of the upper portion of the body (tells more about the man's character) than the lower half. One-third of the time is spent in detailed study of the face. Necktie and collar earn considerable scrutiny, almost as much as the face. There is a tendency to glance up and down the body at least once; however, a different situation exists when we actually meet a person—good manners and habit keep our eyes on the face.

In photographs, the tendency is to focus our attention on a person's eyes more than on any other part of his (or her) face. The reason is obvious: From experience we have learned that eyes mirror one's emotions with fair accuracy. But is this really true? Ocular reactions of the average television viewer show that in this medium it is the lips that receive the closest study. It seems that a moving, active mouth can tell a great deal about a person's mood—and personality. Besides, lip watching helps the audience understand what a person is trying to say.

Merchandise arranged in an orderly manner discourages customers from investigating. They are afraid of destroying the neat pile; guilt feelings associated with childhood experiences keep them from taking the initiative. Nevertheless, well-organized, "quiet" layouts have an important role in advertising. They suggest restrained, dignified, and more self-assured salesmanship. Readers are less apt to identify such layouts with advertising. This is an important point to keep in mind. "Ad-y" gimmicks often weaken the advertiser's message. The average person does not like to be "sold." He prefers to think he is making up his own mind.

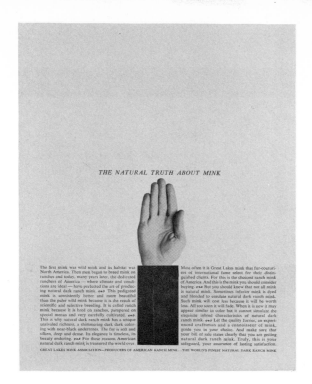

Progressive Grocer Magazine, in its studies of supermarkets, found that "there is something about a jumble of merchandise that seems to pull the shopper to a display and almost compel her to buy. Here's the chance to save; the store hasn't had the time to stock it." Then, too, the customer feels more comfortable about handling, touching, and finally selecting her purchase. She (or he) knows that the display won't be disturbed if an investigation is made of the stock.

The same psychology works in advertising layouts. A deliberately haphazard presentation often encourages the reader to scan the page uninhibitedly. The pell-mell arrangement of items suggests presence of a bargain.

Plenty of "breathing space" lends elegance to these pictures. It is almost impossible to place an expensive piece of merchandise in a cluttered situation and hope to sell it successfully. A luxury item must be given the center of attention.

Every reader (or television viewer) is sensitive to the "mood" of pictures. He may not always realize his own feelings; the average respondent is seldom able to be articulate about such a delicate and complex subject as this. He may be intellectually unaware of it. But this does not mean he does not *feel* its effect.

An outstanding example of selling with "mood" is shown on the left-hand page. This color photograph was used in a magazine advertisement for Lucky Strike to suggest the relaxing aspect of smoking. This kind of unobtrusive advertising can carry a tremendous wallop, its quiet, understated quality notwithstanding.

The two pictures on this page show how mood of pictures can be manipulated by cropping procedures. The tall, vertical photograph gives an illusion of the car's standing still. The horizontal photograph helps to create an illusion of the automobile's moving along the road.

Mood of pictures is determined by many subtle factors. One of them is the subject matter itself, of course, but often this is not the most vital aspect. More important is a photographer's intuitive skill in choosing props, controlling lighting, and finding the right environment in which to display the object. Movie directors have long been aware of these factors, but not advertisers. Businessmen, less cognizant of the "hidden" characteristics that lend pictures a certain atmosphere, still tend to believe that a picture of a rose is a picture of a rose is a picture of a rose. Nothing could be further from the truth.

On the following 11 pages are variations of a single pictorial theme: a chair. Through manipulation of background, the moods of the pictures vary. Like an analyst's patient, the chair goes through a complete change of personality. The magician is photographer Alfred Gescheidt.

elegant

down-to-earth

forlorn

cozy

somber & happy

young

old

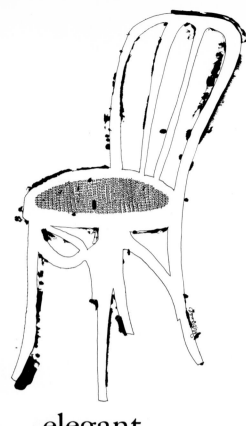

elegant

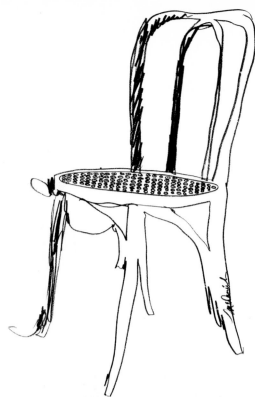

down-to-earth

masculine

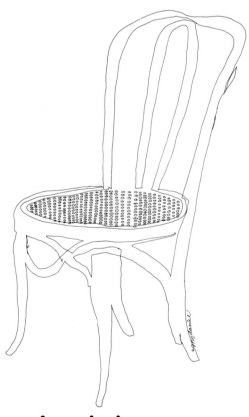

feminine

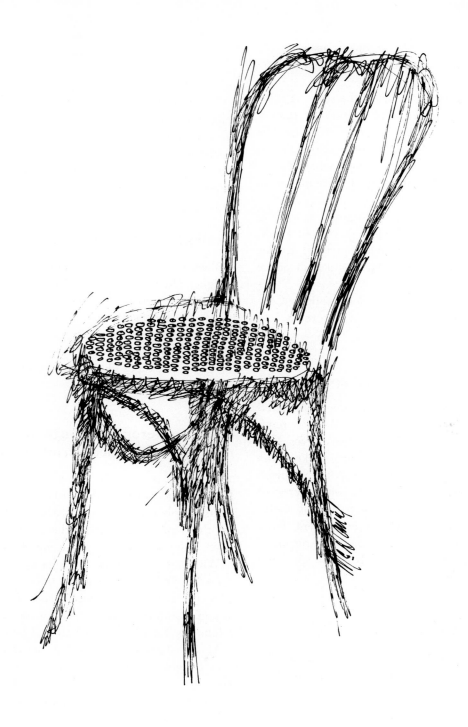

A sensitive artist, just as his friend, the photographer, can also manipulate "mood" in his illustrations. Here Jerry McDaniel, with the help of a pen, pencil, brush, and dexterous hand, shows what happens when he uses a chair as a model for his sketches.

Color attracts more readers. But that isn't all it does.

The dollars invested by an advertiser to show his product in multicolored bloom usually, according to ratings, come back in terms of readership.

But statistics tell only part of the story. A color advertisement is often more *impressive* than a black-and-white version of the same. Photographs shown in their full chromatic glory also make an impact on salesmen, dealers, and wholesalers—the men whose job it is to get the merchandise off the shelves.

Color also helps the reader forget he is looking at a picture. A black-and-white picture of a dish of ice cream is a black-and-white picture. A color photograph of the same subject is a dish of ice cream.

And that isn't all. Color arouses emotions. Contrary to popular belief, color is not related to vision alone.

Each color has a decided connotation.

Some colors are "cold"—like blue, associated with ice—and others are "warm"—like red, reminiscent of fire. As a rule, red also serves as a stimulant; it shakes up the brain, quickens the pulse. Shades of pink suggest festivity. Yellow is energizing, conducive to vitality and a sense of well-being. Green, the color of nature, is soothing and refreshing and abates excitement. Gray is noncommittal and reduces emotional response. Purple—reconciling the far ends of the spectrum —is enigmatic, dramatic.

Colors have odor.

Pale, delicate colors are best associated with flowers. Green often suggests the ozone-filled air of a forest.

Colors have appetite appeal.

Of all the colors, spectrum red (vermilion) seems most appealing; this is the rich color of the apple, the cherry, the rare cut of beef. Red is a favorite color in restaurants and night clubs.

Blue, violet, and purple appear to have little or no appetite appeal. No one has yet succeeded in designing a green bread wrapper that is effective. Tints of blue and violet are decidedly sweet and not for the entrée or filling part of a meal. But peach, orange, buff, and warm yellow titillate the palate effectively.

The color of food packages is probably more important than is generally realized. Customers are profoundly influenced by it. There are hundreds of striking case histories, available in the files of any package or industrial designer, to prove the psychological impact of color.

Colors have weight.

Black is "heavier" than white. Says industrial designer Henry Dreyfuss: "Dark, heavy colors in an airplane give passengers a sense of security. Light colors suggest lack of weight as used for vacuum cleaners to help with their sales." "Weight" considerations become important in designing packages also. People often buy goods on the basis of weight.

Color preferences change according to age, education, income, and locality.

In sunny regions the colors most wanted are likely to be warm and vivid. In more cloudy areas people prefer more conservative hues. During the depression years subdued colors were the rage; today people like vivid, gay hues.

With age, taste in colors change. Small children like yellow; older people prefer it the least. Blue is more for the elderly than for the very young. Children dislike shades of violet, yet adults don't seem to be as strongly averse.

Mass taste is frank, unpretentious. Most people prefer light ("happy") colors to grayish ones, and primary to intermediate ones. Hues are for the more sophisticated people—leaders in style.

The trend is toward increased use of color. People—especially women—are becoming increasingly color conscious. Items that used to come only in black, like automobiles or telephones, now are sold in a multitude of colors. In today's homes, too, even in the kitchen, colors play an important part.

"Second color" (black-and-white plus one color) should be used for emphasis. In their eagerness to get maximum benefit from color, advertisers often apply a second color too lavishly. The result: no visual center of focus, leaving the reader confused.

Color pays off—usually. In displaying food, fashions, or cosmetics, as illustrated here, color is an important part of the story that the advertiser wants to tell. It gives the consumer important information about the product.

But use of color does not *always* bring increased readership. Occasionally a black-and-white picture does just as well. Association with "news" photographs adds credibility to the situation shown here.

4

Sex in advertising

Americans have mixed notions about sex. They are caught between two extreme points of view, both equally convincing. The result: confusion.

Perhaps nowhere in the world is sex stressed as much as in America. To the casual observer it would seem that ours is sexually the most uninhibited nation ever put on the map and that we certainly live in the midst (and not minding a bit) of a highly sensate culture.

There are pictures of female breasts and legs all around us. "Cheesecake" photography has reached new heights in America with statistically impressive results even when compared to the war years when there was roughly one Betty Grable picture for every twelve men in uniform. Publications that make sex their exclusive topic are increasing in both circulation and kind. Movies are getting bluer than ever. The Legion of Decency, which evaluates movies for the guidance of those who care to listen, reports somewhat desperately that "Hollywood has shown an alarming departure from previously accepted and respected standards." It adds, still shaking its collective head, that in 1960 it had to label 24 per cent of movie output "objectionable" as against 14 per cent during the previous year. These movies were announced through a series of posters which, it goes without saying, were equally "objectionable."

There is, of course, nothing wrong with putting emphasis on sex; it helps to propagate the nation and supposedly makes the world a better place in which to live. A problem arises only when the average citizen becomes a target for conflicting theories on sex. Unfortunately, this is what happens in this country. Puritan tradition looks askance at sex. So do a great many mothers and fathers in America. Bombarded with rigid social taboos from one side and highly stimulating displays of seminude women from the other, the hapless Americans become as bewildered as steers in a slaughterhouse. Grasping for help, they flock to the divorce courts by the hundreds, throw themselves on psychiatrists' couches by the thousands, and pick up how-to books on sex by the millions.

If there is anything typical about the sex life of the average American, it is that he goes about it with a great deal of caution.

Sexual furtiveness is as much a part of our culture as blueberry pie. And the advertiser who wants to take advantage of the sensual pulls of sex had better keep in mind this peculiarity of our civilization. In order not to offend his potential customers and to keep their deep-seated inhibitions more or less in order, the advertiser must assure his audience—by implication or by blunt statement—that sex really isn't so bad after all.

Why use sex in advertising at all?

The advertiser may ask: "Why not leave sex alone then?" The answer is simple. There are few appeals in advertising that equal the force of sex. Readership studies show that here is one element that arouses the immediate interest of *both* men and women. Perhaps, not surprisingly, sex has the greatest universal acceptance of all stratagems ever used in advertising.

Even more important are the "hidden"—unconscious—feelings that sex arouses in the audience. It might be well to mention some of these:

1. Sex makes the beholder feel young again.
2. Sex reassures men of their masculinity, women of their femininity. In today's confused relationship between men and women, this reassurance is an important consideration.
3. Sex is one of the most basic of all human emotions. It offers a means of "getting away from it all." Strong, healthy sexual drive is as uncomplicated a release of one's energies as, for example, the meeting of a new business acquaintance at a cocktail party is not.
4. Sex is a status symbol. To the American public glamour represents an achievement per se. With good-looks go the rights of those who are superior. The simplest way for an advertiser to give his models an air of importance is to bestow them with sex appeal.

Man's idea of sex is typically his. This illustration pleases the male audience, which tends to think of sex primarily in terms of a physical adventure.

Women draw a thin line between sex and romance. The Tabu advertisement is effective because it has an aura of emotions other than the purely sexual.

I dreamed I was a vamp
in my *maidenform* bra

What a fabulous flashback! I'm a slinky siren of the thirties—in my SWEET MUSIC* *long-line* bra! Made of heavenly alençon lace. *Melts* away my midriff. *Feels* as lyrically lovely as it looks (two panels of sheer elastic at the back for blissful breathing comfort)! White and black B, C cups, 5.95. D, 6.95. (SWEET MUSIC also in white *broadcloth*, B, C cups, 3.95; D, 4.95.)

This Maidenform advertisement—part of a campaign that became a classic success story in the field—shows that it is possible to present sex in its most basic form, if properly ensconced in an atmosphere of fantasy, to a mass female audience. This situation, the kind that women unconsciously would like to experience, is made acceptable by converting it into a dream, where no woman can be held responsible for her actions. To make its dream girls more agreeable to the virtuous females, Maidenform ads feature only *white* brassières. Shown on the opposite page is a more direct approach to sex. Miss Pickle is an appropriate symbol for male admirers who associate sex with living it up. Less friendly are the feelings between Miss Pickle and the Women of America.

NATIONAL
PICKLE
WEEK
MAY 21·30

Research shows that the display of sex is a forceful attention-getter. But figures can be misleading.

Cheesecake photography almost invariably gets high noting in magazine and newspaper pages. It also gets—and holds—the rapt attention of television viewers. However, a note of warning: The advertiser should not think that just because he sold his girl he has sold his product.

There are indications that this type of interest often stops exactly where it started, i.e., sex. The experience of coupon advertising sponsored by Rotolite copying machine offers convincing evidence. The advertisement on top (*a*) received high noting but only 52 coupon returns. When the picture of the girl in a bathing suit was changed to a more relevant cartoon treatment of the subject at hand (*b*), replies jumped to 109.

Television advertisers frequently have similar experiences with a model that makes viewers react with a sigh. What she says sometimes becomes less important than what she does. Apparently she does manage to get a captive audience; men watch her closely, thoughts cross their minds, but few that concern the product. Even more detrimental is the reaction of the female audience. Sensing competition, they are apt to call her anything but her proper name. Sensuous beauty has been many a fine commercial narrator's undoing. Today almost all successful "pitch" women are attractive, but they are hardly the type that would appear on top of calendars.

The important thing is not to flaunt sex appeal too openly. Beauty is still a great asset to women announcers. On the right-hand page is an example of how exuberant attractiveness can be toned down by a simple adjustment of the neckline.

Sex can hurt the advertiser's image.

Sometimes the use of sex in advertising will get excellent and immediate results. In the long run, however, it can damage a sponsor's reputation. Apparently, a great many women (and men, too) associate sex with a multitude of sins. This approach may be all right if the advertiser is selling a movie or a book but not if he is trying to build up a solid company image with his stockholders.

a

b

Environment in which sex is presented will often deeply influence women's reactions.

Above is a photograph of a night-club entertainer bursting forth in song. She has a great deal of sex appeal which she is not trying to hide with her attire. Yet few women will resent this picture, whether they are married or unmarried. The surroundings here are elegant, suggesting a high level of entertainment. More significantly, the singer is not available to the male listeners with their female companions. The sight of her may be sexually exciting to the men, but after the show is over, the chances are good that the men will leave their tables with the same women they came in with. There is therefore little danger of competition here.

Not so with the documentary picture on the right. This kind of rough-and-ready depiction of sex, shown at its realistic best, makes women apprehensive. The back view of the woman, the appearance of the man at the door leave little doubt as to the purpose of this meeting.

From Petti of Encino: The swim shape in cotton sharkskin. Adjustable front lacing, inner bra-styling. Turquoise only. Sizes 5 to 15, about $17. PETTI OF ENCINO, A DIVISION OF GLEN MANUFACTURING INC., 1407 BROADWAY, NEW YORK 18, NEW YORK. PETTI BY VAL HUGHES · MONTREAL, CANADA.

An interesting demonstration shows that under certain conditions a direct, no-nonsense approach to sex can appeal even to a female audience. In the "tip of her tongue is the Petti" campaign, girls in highly provocative stances were featured. What was on their minds apparently was primarily sex. Some of the more prudish readers resented such an open show of base instincts (and a few stores refused to carry Petti sweaters) but all in all the campaign proved to be a great success.

These pictures do not conform to the traditional cheesecake approach to sex. The girl, in spite of her knowing look, does not appear to be the kind who would let herself be too indiscreet. There is a suggestion of clean, natural animal sex appeal here, displayed with a frankness that helps to dispel any feelings of guilt. This girl has no inhibitions; she values sex highly but does not take herself too seriously. Women—though they do not always admit it—will readily identify themselves with such a person.

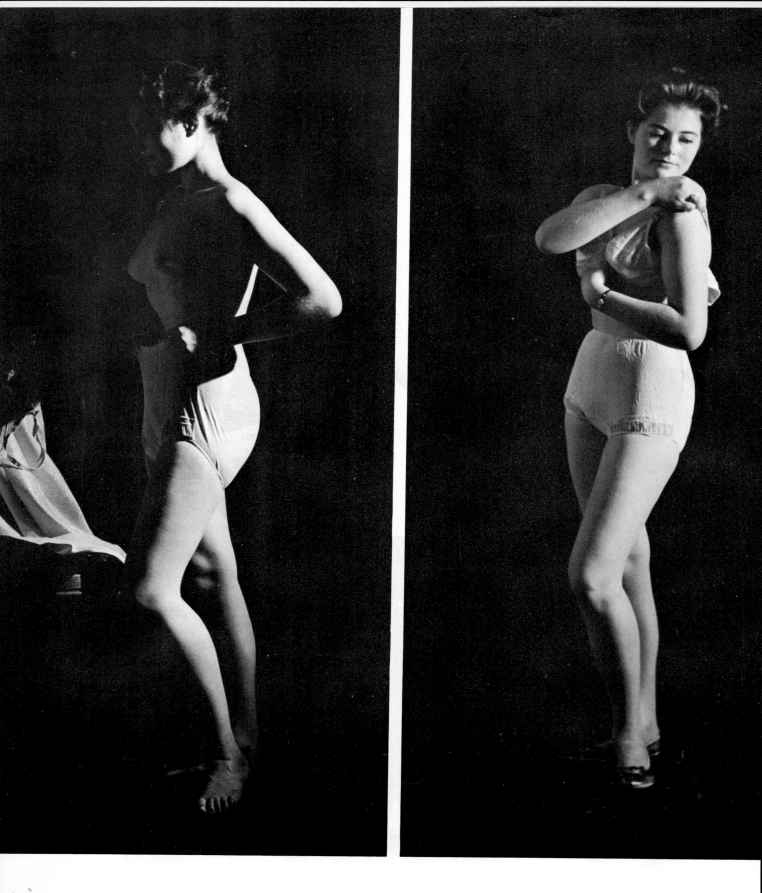

Girl donning her clothes—a striptease in reverse—shows that she ca

...ok as desirable (and sometimes more so) fully dressed as in the nude.

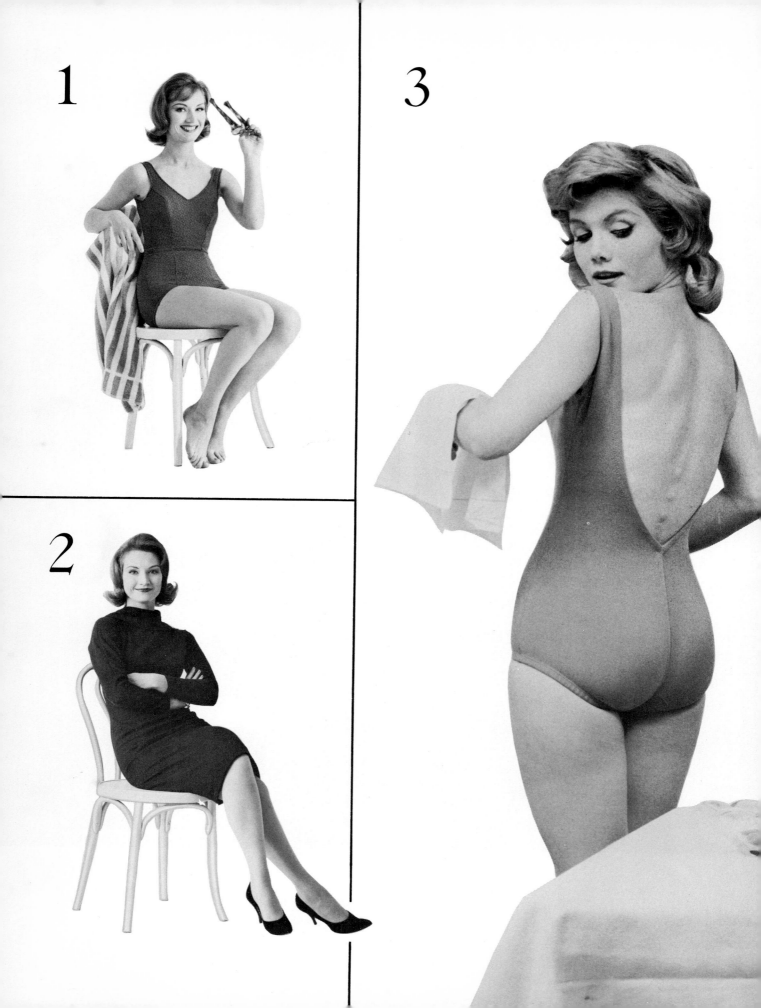

Ample display of the female body, such as a girl in a bathing suit, does not necessarily hold out more promise of sex than same person fully clothed (1 and 2). But put her in an environment where her attire is not what the beholder would expect (3) and there can be no doubt about her increased sex appeal.

almost all the great shapes on
the beach are created by **Cole**
of California

©1959 Cole of California

Our shapes, (left to right): the slim shift under the Empire coat, printed Dacron®-and-cotton. Suit, $14.95. Set, $25. The camisole
sheath, striped Empire-high; in Chromspun® lastex, $25. The balloon, a pouf of printed cotton satin over a matching sheath; suit,
$17.95; set, $25. All by Cole's own genius, designer Margit Fellegi. *And* with Cole's own secret: Power Profile, shapeliest bra a-float.

Another example shows that a woman's nude body—such as one would see in a
nudist camp—will not necessarily make men look twice. Shown above is an
advertisement sponsored by Cole of California. The sight of a completely nude
woman in this line-up caused few raised eyebrows. The photograph on the left,
on the other hand, leaves everything to the reader's imagination; the body of
the model is not physically present on the page. Yet, the photograph, done for
Peter Pan swimwear, breathes sex appeal.

—and other factors:

brics have sexual contations. Wool is the ast feminine of the ur materials shown on e opposite page. It akes the woman apar businesslike, urban, phisticated.

Linen has a mixed image. If it is white, the fabric strongly suggests purity. It is more feminine than wool but has little seductive power. Linen is associated with clean, wholesome fun.

The delicacy (and lightness) of lace makes it very much a woman's fabric. Rich in pattern, lace exudes an air of elegance, aloofness, yet soft femininity.

Silk is the most sensuous of all materials. It shines and reflects the play of light. It is very soft and clings to a woman's body. This characteristic makes silk (or satin) bring out the seductive qualities of its wearer.

The picture of the girl resting on wood has the least sex appeal of the three shown on the opposite page. The floor is too hard, and it appears to be uncomfortable.

The same model languishing on a mattress, her head on a pillow, promises rich sexual opportunities. However, this picture will provoke guilt feelings in many people.

The same girl wearing different types of sweaters shows that the sex appeal of tight outfits is not the same as that of loose, oversized ones. The former suggests a provocative, more direct approach to sex. The latter appeals more to those who like good sportsmanship and a sunny disposition.

A more "natural" approach to sex is suggested (subconsciously) in the photograph of a girl relaxing outdoors. This picture is less apt to induce complicated inhibitions in the beholder; it makes him feel more at ease.

What has the girl's attitude to do with her sex appeal?

There are girls whose presence brings to mind lifelong companionship, a big family, a house in the suburbs. Then there are those, equally attractive, who evoke a different kind of image, such as a pleasurable evening spent in a night club.

The girl on the left typifies the kind of wholesome effervescence that most males would like to perpetuate in their wives. She is the outdoor type, straightforward, unaffected, guileless, and simple at heart. If there is a "typical American girl," this tall, slender woman comes close to embodying her. This girl is the marrying kind. She is not a "date"; she is a potential wife.

The appeal of the girl on the right is based on different attributes. While the one who so prettily fills up the opposite page is clearly the sort who would be *liked* by one and all, the blonde on the right demands more than just being the most popular girl in the class. She wants, and asserts her claim boldly, to be *desired*. And as anyone past puberty knows, there are some important differences between the physical assertion of liking or loving a person.

It is important to realize when taking photographs of models that their sex appeal depends largely on their *attitude*. Almost any girl can play the role of a sultry damsel if she cares to. The two girls on these pages could easily switch parts. Only their mode of dressing would be different and, of course, their expressions.

Which "type" is the advertiser's best girl friend?

Either girl may serve the advertiser's interest in selling his product, depending on the kind of impression he is trying to make on his audience. The young lady with the less inhibited outlook on life (judging from her picture) may be just the right choice for a cosmetic or a sports car manufacturer, but most likely not the one for selling a breakfast cereal to Mom, Pop, and all the kids.

Again, it should be emphasized that people have as varied reactions to sex as to politics and religion. Few men (or women) agree on what constitutes the "ideal" female.

Fit for any figure—stretch-nylon lace!

Stardust has whipped up something provocative in the way of lacy lingerie. Consider this slip. The top part is made of an extraordinary new fabric: Helanca® stretch lace of Chemstrand nylon by Liberty. This means that the beautiful lace bodice molds itself to the bra underneath to fit every figure perfectly. The result is a very tidy silhouette. Slip of satiny nylon tricot with a band of non-stretch lace (for prettiness) around the hem. Sizes 32 to 40. About $4.00.

Chemstrand® nylon

CHEMSTRAND MAKES ONLY THE YARN. AMERICA'S FINEST MILLS AND MANUFACTURERS DO THE REST.

THE CHEMSTRAND CORPORATION, 350 FIFTH AVE., N. Y. 1 • PLANTS: CHEMSTRAND® NYLON—PENSACOLA, FLA. • ACRILAN® ACRYLIC FIBER—DECATUR, ALA.

Another pictorial testimony shows that it is what appears to be on the girl's mind that gives her a special sex appeal. The model on the left-hand page, displaying lingerie, performs her duty with a great deal of charm. Her blithe movements, dainty figure, and enchanting smile suggest—above all—coyness. The girl in the Chemstrand advertisement approaches the subject of sex directly. Her seductive pose is not only cute, it is highly beguiling.

In lingerie advertising the merchandise can be displayed seductively. Details in workmanship of the slip are important, but so is the buyer's subconscious admission that lacy lingerie (unlike a girdle or for some women a brassière) is more than just a functional garment.

Stripe it rich...

Cone's exciting new SPANGLES towel brings a new glamour into your private life. Delight in its cheerful play of color-with-color, in exuberant stripes. Luxuriate in the fluffy softness of its lofty loop construction... plus Cone's exclusive "Wondasoft" finish, that is so lovely to touch. And the colors are woven in to last... brightly, beautifully. In shades of Gold-and-Topaz, Violet-and-Turquoise, Brown-and-Pink, all on white. And less expensive than you think: the full-bodied, full-sized, cotton bath towel about **$1**. Guest towel about **59¢**. Wash cloth about **39¢**.

Be sure to ask for the fabulous LINT-FREE KITCHEN TERRIES. Speedy-drying cotton terry towels in a wide selection of handsome patterns — their yarn-dyed colors woven in to stay. Only **39¢** and **59¢**.

"Makers of fine quality towels and terry cloth"

CONE IS THE FOR TOWELS

CONE MILLS INC., 1440 Broadway, New York City

M MARTEX® Couturier look for the bath...'Paris Skies' by Martex.

B. F.'s WIFE WEARS B. H. WRAGGE

And doesn't she look as if B. F. were the chairman of the board. This winter she heads for Jamaica in a handwoven silk suit with years of wear ahead. Natural color only. 79.95. Above: Floating skirt over a slender shaft of silk linen. Gold, lime, black or orange. 69.95. Lower left: Stove pipe pants and jacket in handwoven silk from India. Blouse in a lighter weight of the same fabric. Natural color silk only. Pants, 39.95. Jacket, 65.00. Blouse, 29.95. All in 8-16 sizes.

The brand new B. H. Wragge Resort Collection is arriving this second at all Bonwit Teller Stores, Neiman-Marcus, I. Magnin & Co. and the J. L. Hudson Co.

Frequently the advertiser would like to imply the presence of sex in his ad but do so in the best possible taste. In cases like this, it may be well to consider a means by which to *lessen* the sex appeal of the models in the illustration.

Two towel advertisements on the opposite page show how the introduction of a little girl into the picture can make the model sexually less inspiring. Unlike the model with black stockings in the Martex ad (a photograph that is nonetheless executed in excellent taste), the girl covered with the Cone towel leaves one with the impression that she has already been spoken for. The same situation is suggested even more convincingly in the highly successful B. H. Wragge campaign. It was found that the effectiveness of the ads was increased by including a provocative photograph of a girl (shown in blow-up) accompanied by candid shots of her day as a *wife* and business woman.

On this page are shown two other means by which a woman's figure may be made less sexually exciting.

5

The charm of being old-fashioned

A hankering for the "good old days" is a favorite pastime for many.

There are a great number of people who earnestly claim that the present is no improvement over the past nor will the future be any better. Parents often try to pass this interesting belief along to their children, only to get a shoulder-shrugging reply about "the older generation that lives in the past." Not too many years later, these children grow up and tend to do the same thing with the young members of *their* family.

It is difficult to understand the logic behind all this commemoration. Civilization, after all, tends to move forward, not backward. Working hours are getting shorter, homes are becoming more comfortable, more money is available to more people, the populace is better educated, medical science is marching forward, and men and women are getting healthier, taller, stronger. It is hard to believe rationally that the "good old days" were really as good as they are reputed to have been.

Why, then, does the past seem so enticing?

The tendency to want to "go back" into the past (while also insisting on moving forward) is based on feelings common in all humans. Like so many of our emotions, these desires have little to do with logic.

1. Childhood memories have a way of picking up drama as the individual grows older. He talks about his "happy childhood." In a way, he never had it so good; this is true. This was the period in his life when he was more or less taken care of. There is a desire in all of us to return to this blessed state of affairs. Psychologists call this tendency—in extreme cases—"infantile retrogression." Objects, people, events which become associated with these days tend to take on a happy coloring.

2. Universal, too, is the predilection to repress what is unpleasant and to bring forward only what is pleasant. Thus we are all the more apt to recall the happy incidents of our childhood. These memories stick with us for the rest of our lives with incredible tenacity.

3. The older an individual gets, the more he worries about his loss of vigor, energy, and youthful enthusiasm. There is plenty of evidence that this feeling is unrealistic (we develop other assets to replace the old ones), but nevertheless it is there. In effect a person somewhat along in years usually wishes he were young again and, not too surprisingly, recalls his earlier days as the best of his life.

Can an advertiser afford to be "old-fashioned"?

The human inclination to find charm in the produce of bygone days sometimes gives an advertiser a valuable tool by which to sell his wares. In such industries as food, toys, home furnishings, and gift items (especially around Christmas) nostalgia is closely related to the individual's desire to buy. Parents have a special feeling for toys they knew as children (balls, rocking horses, and dolls are perennial best-sellers). Candy manufacturers like to pack their goodies in boxes that show scenes associated with happy memories. In its hundred and seventieth year, *The Old Farmer's Almanac* still sells over a million copies with each publication. Some advertising campaigns (like Breck's shown on opposite page) are based on "old-fashioned" virtues.

The use of old-fashioned graphic artifices does not necessarily make the advertiser seem "old-fashioned." Actually, the average reader tends to associate these devices more with charm than backward-mindedness. As it happens, some of the most modern layouts make liberal use of old type faces, props, and even illustrations.

The advertiser must make sure, however—instinct will tell him—that the reader understands the reasons for using old-fashioned designs. They should always serve the purpose of *deliberately* trying to establish an atmosphere of yesterday, borrowing from the many excellent artistic expressions of those days. If the reader senses that the advertiser is enveloping his message in out-of-date clothing only because he does not know any better, then that's a different story. For this reason, it is probably a less risky undertaking to borrow a gimcrack devised two centuries ago than one only twenty years old.

1888:

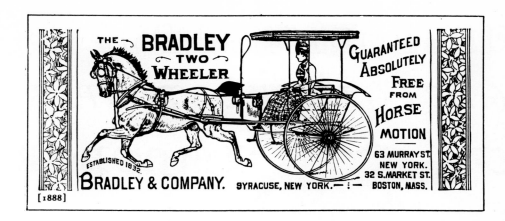

1927:

1960:

"Old" type faces provide the artist with a wealth of inspiration. Some are too ornate for our modern sense of design. But the exuberant charm which is part of so much of yesteryear's art form makes up for its shortcomings. We tend to associate these type faces with pleasant memories. They have the warmth that some of the modern type faces (for example, Futura) lack. There is little problem in tastefully lumping together these type faces on a page; each has a design so unique, so eccentric, that, when put in juxtaposition, the result seems to be an uninhibited hodgepodge of artistic endeavor with an appeal all its own.

Even some of the most modern corporations today use "old-fashioned" techniques in their advertising without hurting their image.

It all depends on the way it is done. On the left-hand page are a few examples of some highly successful television commercials put on to sell the process of the Sanforized Division of Cluett, Peabody & Company. There is obviously nothing new about this commercial—Mack Sennett invented the pie-in-the-face, pratfall, rolling-eye approach almost half a century ago—and yet the total effect is up to date. The very fact that such a technique is used in a television commercial and that it is shown here as well makes it something "new."

When and if an advertiser chooses to apply such a method to his advertising, he must be careful that his execution follows the subtleties that give such performances their special flavor; otherwise, the results will be neither fish nor fowl. The film shown here has been prepared with painstaking care. The French movie company Remont haunted the Paris Cinéma for months and saw that institution's complete file of old American movies, including a number made by Mr. Sennett's company. After sitting through the old movies several times, they were able to capture the motions and actions of the Sennett actors so that their productions could duplicate visually the quality of the old silents. Because modern cameras work at 24 frames a second, the jerky action of the old film was simulated by eliminating half the frames. Although the film was shot in black and white, it was reproduced on color film to give the finished product the blue-gray tone of the silent films. Background music consisted of bittersweet piano music.

On the right side of this page are a few reproductions of newspaper pages, each using an "old-fashioned" approach. Do *they* look old-fashioned today? They probably do. But the *advertisement* in which they appear does not.

Some pictures evoke sentiments the source of which is not too easy to determine. This photograph depicts a commonplace occurrence: cows pasturing on farmland. Soft, diffused handling of the subject, however, summons forth long-forgotten memories about similar pictures we saw many years ago. A corresponding technique used in a "modern" picture would have nostalgic connotations.

The brush (above) with the "elegantly mounted and carved back" features a fanciful pattern that could only have been conceived in the heyday of the Victorian period. It ignores practically all rules of sound design. Yet today even this item exudes charm just as do many antiques which in their day were on the border line of good taste. Time improves the appearance of things.

Combining antiques with modern pieces (right) "softens" the total effect. Interior decorators (and housewives) are getting less inhibited about "mixing periods." So are commercial photographers, who display modern merchandise in old-fashioned surroundings.

Family life of yesteryear is fondly remembered by many. In those days, it is said, families were more closely knit. Father was the undisputed head of the house while mother spent her time in maintaining the home for one and all. Illustrations depicting a similar state of affairs in the milieu of a modern family (like in some of the drawings of Norman Rockwell) have an amazingly wide appeal.

Here, too, rational explanations cover up underlying emotions. Depth interviews reveal that it is not so much the "old order of family life" per se that the individual wants but that he longs for the way things used to be when he was a child. The virtues a husband wants in his wife bear close resemblance to those his father wanted in *his* spouse. The demands he makes on his children are often the same as those made on him when he was young.

Be that as it may, the moral rectitude, the spirit of old-fashioned family life, strikes a responsive chord in millions of hearts. This is especially true of those living in the rural areas and the Midwestern and Southern states and of the less-educated and the middle-income groups.

OUT

6

How to make the viewer feel a part of the picture: a study of empathy

The term *empathy,* as used by psychologists, means "imaginative projection of one's own consciousness into another human being." This phenomenon has been found to be very strong. We see empathy at work in individuals, singly and collectively, day after day all around us. Charity drives would never reach their goals if people were unable to imagine themselves in someone else's place. The immense power of soap operas is based on this human inclination; viewer identification with favorite heroes and heroines manifests itself in the thousands of letters received daily by the networks. The success of movies, fiction published in women's magazines, comic strips, biographical sketches, and television commercials trying to dispense headache pills can be retraced to this propensity to experience emotions of others.

Certain feelings are as old as mankind.

When trying to find pictures that will have a wide appeal, one must keep in mind the important fact that people are *basically* very much alike in their emotions. By touching the heart, some illustrations receive the same reactions from poor and rich, men or women, young or old, highbrow and lowbrow, Bushman or Texas oil magnate.

On the most basic level—starting at infancy—are such pervasive drives as hunger, need for sleep, instinct for sex, need for companionship, search for approval, drive toward activity, and at the same time, desire for comfort.

As we mature, our prime urges find more intricate expressions; a conflict exists between what we would like to do (libido) and what others make us do (superego), and things become a bit more complicated. We find new outlets for fulfilling our innate desire for approval; we learn to compete, "keep up with the Joneses," excel in various areas and be praised for it. With our parents more or less out of our lives, we look for an authority substitute: job, boss, God. We develop the ability to love. We learn ways to avoid trouble, deal with people, watch our health, raise a family, take on responsibility. Still the basic needs are there, as they always were, clamoring for recognition as insistently as ever. *Our methods of fulfilling these needs change, but not the needs themselves.* Once we understand this psychological truism, we will have little difficulty in selecting the kind of pictures that speak everybody's language.

Increased emotional involvement will occur under the following circumstances:

1. If the situation depicted represents a familiar scene to the viewer.

Discovering things he "knows" (a baseball stadium, a picnic, children playing in a haystack) will abate the average person's apprehension of entering into a situation. Even if the activity in the picture appears strange to him at first glance, he may, on second perusal, find he can imagine himself in the situation presented, provided there is enough in the background with which he can identify.

2. If he likes the people in the scene.

The choice of models plays an important part in making the pictures enticing. If the people presented appear friendly to the reader, then he will be able to act as imaginary host. If he does not like their appearance, he will unconsciously want to stay out and not identify. Thus a small-town businessman looking at a picture of a theatre audience at a ballet may more readily relate himself to a spectator *if* he discovers that the girl sitting in the adjoining seat reminds him of the one he used to take to the corner drugstore for a soda. Conversely, a girl unskilled in sports may be quite willing to imagine herself standing on skis at the top of a mountain *if* there happens to be a man in the illustration who looks like the type who would help her in distress.

Readership studies show that there is a strong tendency for the individual to identify himself with people younger than he. When confronted with pictures of groups of men and women having a party, the elderly reader compares himself in the illustration not with someone close to his vintage but with one considerably his junior.

Attractive girls in pictures usually get their men: the readers. Married or single, tall or short, rich or poor, most male readers seem to have little trouble in visualizing themselves standing next to a lovely lady. Curiously enough, the oldest readers usually go for the youngest damsel in the illustration.

3. If the picture does not evoke unfavorable associations.

Insurance companies found out a long time ago that pictures of grieving widows surrounded by hungry children were not the most forceful way of persuading readers to take out life insurance. There is a strong instinct on the part of most people to want to stay clear of predicaments. Psychological jargon refers to this avoidance of unhappy situations as the "pleasure principle." Illustrations suggesting happy, positive events (as a general rule) encourage more readership.

The lengths to which readers will go to avoid situations that hold out even the remotest possibility of trouble is indeed amazing. A television commercial featuring a stern, middle-aged woman (but with a kind heart) kept some viewers from listening to her message because of an association with a teacher from their long-forgotten past. Advertisements featuring abstract art often fail to get hoped-for readership, not because of a lack of communication, but rather because of a latent reluctance to become involved with anything so unfamiliar as to cause possible social embarrassment.

4. If there is nothing in the picture that goes against his (or her) moral convictions.

Many people are willing to change their opinions on subjects they consider of minor importance, but it is nearly impossible to produce new feelings about significant issues by means of a few advertisements. In the first place, the average reader resents being sold and lectured both at the same time. Anyway, he will, by virtue of being human, tenaciously cling to his principles about religion, politics, Americanism, hard work, motherhood, and not too infrequently child raising, performances of various automobiles, and drinking. These issues are often accompanied by potent emotions of which the individual may be blissfully ignorant. If he feels that his beliefs are being threatened, he will either leave the scene (i.e., the illustration) entirely or resent it with active anger. Empathic reaction in this case is not forthcoming.

For this reason many excellent pictures fail commercially. Illustrations which show groups of people are often coolly received in certain circles in Southern and Midwestern regions of the country. Rarely successful is an advertisement that even remotely suggests the presence of a gambling activity. A photograph of a church picnic will do better if the spire in the background is fuzzy enough to hide the religious denomination of the building. Too, the political convictions of the people in an illustration is best left to conjecture.

Again, it should be understood that a reader's reluctance to become part of a picture which goes against his moral grain is seldom a conscious reaction. Rather it is automatic. He may turn the page or block out the television commercial from his consciousness before the advertiser ever has a chance to fully present his case.

5. If he doesn't have to change much in the picture.

Situations that might imply work on the viewer's part (such as dishes waiting to be washed or an empty room needing furniture or possibly a queue in front of a ticket window) as a rule make the reader turn away. The anticipation of completing chores or making an effort is distasteful to him.

6. If there is a promise that his desires will be fulfilled.

Usually there is hardly any problem of involving the reader with the picture if there is something he needs or thinks he needs presented. This could be a platter with a sizzling steak, an automobile waiting to be driven out of the showroom, a pretty girl expecting her date, a house by the beach.

7. If there is somebody in the illustration the viewer would like to be.

Male readers easily identify themselves with dynamic, successful men in pictures. Women like to fancy themselves in the place of the glamour girls who seem to be having such gay times in advertising illustrations and television commercials. With an eye on these heroes and heroines, the average person sometimes indulges in Walter Mitty adventures that help him in finding temporary escape from the problems of reality. A dramatic demonstration of this tendency is offered by studies made by *Fortune* magazine. Although the topics taken up by this publication primarily affect those people with incomes of over $50,000, the readership consists mostly of young men making less than $20,000 annually. Among the best-read features in *Time* magazine are case histories concerning the fortunate individuals (their age given) who became rich before reaching middle age.

Most women readers are apt to feel more at home in the picture on the left. There is a feeling of warm, genuine companionship there; here is a fun-loving group that would quickly make a stranger feel comfortable. And most important: Not all girls in the picture live up to the stereotyped idea of glamour. Research studies show that many female readers instinctively beat a retreat when confronted with a roomful of beauties.

The superlatively executed portrait picture (on top) of fashionable ladies gets close scrutiny from women but little empathy. The mood of expansive elegance and the aloof mien of the models limit the interest to merchandise (jewelry and clothes). The reader remains a spectator and does not become an active participant.

Humans are profoundly susceptible to the emotions, moods, and actions of others. The smile is one of the first responses made by an infant to his environment. Later, he learns to react to a variety of stimuli.

Visual communicators take advantage of our vicarious nature by showing happy people to make one more cheerful, sad faces to create a more contemplative mood, excited groups to arouse one's curiosity.

Airlines have always shown a marked predilection for angle shots in advertising their prize commodity: the airplane. Studies have indicated that the public is not so much preoccupied with the machinery of the transport; pictures of the interiors of these winged miracles are more reassuring and interesting to them.

Ocean-liner companies, too, are seldom able to resist the temptation to show full views of their floating palaces. Such pictures can be an impressive sight, but again the advertiser must remember that readers are more interested in the fun they will have aboard than in the tonnage of the ship. Both pictures shown here display the magnificence of the ship, but the one on the opposite page exudes an atmosphere of gaiety as well.

Another demonstration of how the "pleasure principle" works in travel advertising. Illustrations showing people boarding a plane or ship usually have lower readership than those depicting scenes of landing. The fun of anticipating the arrival is very real. For this reason, the advertising campaign prepared for the American Export Lines (right-hand page) was psychologically sound. Illustrations suggest that the ship is already at the point of destination.

Sight-see your way to Europe on the Sunlane. On the Sunlane, you see more than the sea, You sail through the green-carpeted Azores and past the African coast, with its snowy peaks. You see Algeciras (port for Madrid), a quaint Spanish town nestling beside Gibraltar. Next, Cannes, the glittering French Riviera (only hours to Paris!), Genoa and Portofino, part fishing port, part Paradise (pictured above). You sweep into Naples; can you really be seeing Vesuvius? And—the air is warm, the ship is magnificent, the ocean is relaxed. Ask your travel agent. **CONSTITUTION & INDEPENDENCE·American Export Lines**

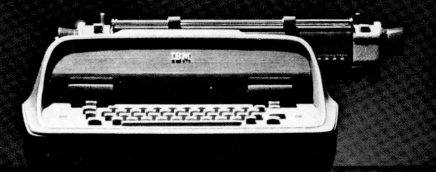

Do not put people in advertisements only for the sake of injecting "human interest" into the picture. The mere presence of a human being does not necessarily make an ad more interesting. Of all typewriter campaigns, the solitary (and dramatic) display of the IBM machines has proved to get the highest consistent readership. Typewriters shown in their natural setting, the office, usually get only average noting. A sole typewriter suggests newness (it hasn't been used yet) and invites one to try it out.

Which of the two photographs on top would be likely to receive more readership? Probably the one on the right. Insertion of a pretty girl is little help here. Studies show that a viewer is more willing to "step into" an empty room as opposed to one that "belongs" to someone else—as the presence of the girl suggests in this case. The sight of a crowded room reminds the reader of going to a party at a friend's house. An empty room, on the other hand, is more like one's own home —quiet and undisturbed.

One of the most successful campaigns ever conceived in the home-furnishing industry is sponsored by the Armstrong Cork Company. Rarely is a person shown in the photograph. Meticulous attention is given to details (other than its own product, the floor), and the decorating ideas provide great interest. Often as many as three-quarters of all readers questioned notice these ads.

Readers like to think of themselves doing pleasant tasks. They want to consider the *results* of their labor, not the effort involved. Rarely do pictures of homeowners installing flooring, acoustical ceilings, insulation, or roofing attract as high reader interest as do those showing the end result of one's toils—a completed room or house.

Pictures of food rank high in terms of readership. Only department store ads can compete with the inherent interest of food advertising. Recipes in advertisements, no matter how small the print, get read, clipped, and filed away.

The illustrations shown on these two pages demonstrate various points of pictorializing food products. Here again, a photograph of a housewife at work (a) produces less empathic involvement—even though there is "human interest"—than the showing of the finished result: an appetizing dish. Many women claim they enjoy cooking, but depth interviews clearly indicate that it isn't so much the toil in the kitchen they like but rather the impending reward of their output of energy: the praise they get (or hope for) from husbands, children, and guests.

Photographs that induce the association of food with its odor usually do well (b). Smell plays an important part in creating hunger pangs. The pungent aroma of brewing coffee, the sweet scent of apple pie, the smoky essence of a broiled steak are pleasant accompaniments to food itself.

The most effective visualizations of food—in terms of advertising—are those that titillate the reader's palate. What we eat, after all, is still selected primarily on the basis of taste. Special care must be taken to display food in an appetizing manner (c).

Memories of the mealtime ritual revert to our childhood. Because these recollections usually bring forth pleasurable associations, the tendency is to cling to them. There is a marked resistance toward certain changes. When a bakery tried to change the shape of its loaf of wheat bread from round to square, sales dropped (d).

Setting a table is a form of art to a woman, an expression of her personality (e). She takes pride in her skill. For this reason, food shown on the table, attractively served, usually does exceptionally well in female readership.

Eating is a social affair (f). The enjoyment of food itself is only part of the fun; just as important is the fact that mealtime affords an opportunity to make social contacts and carry on a relaxed conversation. Dinnertime is also strongly associated with the gathering of the family—mother, father, children. That is why so many people think of this time of the day with feelings of love, warmth, and closeness.

a

b

c

e

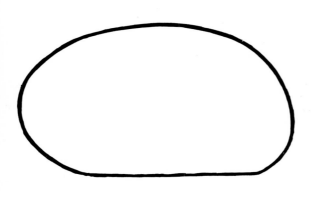

d

f

INSTANT

The commercial for Johnson's Baby Powder (left-hand page) shows the use of a product from a mother's point of view. Visual devices like these make it easy for the viewer to identify herself (or himself) with the situation. The same principle (user does not appear at all) is used in the Tang commercial.

Lonely girl basking in the sun, sitting self-contentedly, arouses male interest. Implied here is an opportunity for a man to strike up a conversation with her and make a social contact. There's no one in the background to interfere. This photograph would attract both men and women readers.

This lady observing herself in the mirror would discourage the average male reader from getting involved. She is too busy putting on make-up, a feminine occupation that excludes male participation. The picture would attract the interest only of women.

Photograph of strong man, full of "masculine" symbols (tattooed hand, bald head, skyscraper background), nonetheless gets feminine attention. The atmosphere of masculinity in the Marlboro cigarette ads helped to increase sales among *both* sexes. This is the kind of man with whom women would like to be seen.

Less feminine interest is aroused by this picture. Though displaying an impressive set of biceps and an even richer array of tattoo marks than the Marlboro man, this gentleman suggests too much brawn and not enough brain. The picture represents man-to-man communication.

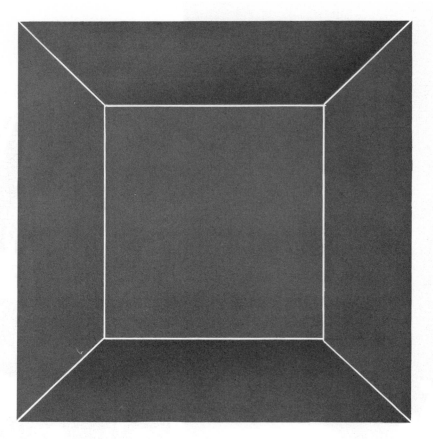

Some shapes beckon the viewer to enter. This three-dimensional illustration of the inside of a cube allows the beholder to "step in." Pictures on television that move *away* have the same beckoning quality; moving *toward* the viewer, they make him instinctively draw back.

One-dimensional square suggests an impenetrable wall. It does not invite the reader to enter; rather, it seems to tell him to stay out.

Dark colors tend to look heavy and imperviable.

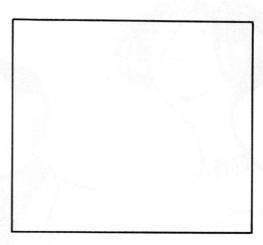

Light colors seem to have more lucidity, encouraging the viewer to come inside.

(*Above*) Spiral lines suggest a vortex, drawing its subjects in close toward its center.

(*Right*) Warm colors seem inviting to the viewer, cold colors keep him out. Red has a quality of friendliness. Blue connotes a quality of aloofness, dignity. Green is neither inviting nor unfriendly.

"I don't know—vodka and something."

"Light on the soda, pal."

"Don't bother about me. I know where you keep it."

Saxon

"What is everybody else having?"

"Are you sure this is Scotch? I only drink Scotch."

"Bourbon."

We tend to associate ourselves quickly with anything that represents a familiar scene. On the right is a photograph of a young boy running through a corn field. This situation evokes a favorable childhood memory, joys of living on a farm or roaming through the fields. Shown above are cartoonist Charles Saxon's perceptive sketches of suburbanites. The types are depicted so accurately that they are instantly recognized as people we know or may have known at one time. Hence the impact of his illustrations.

Candid photographs like the one above (taken for Lucky Strike cigarettes) make the reader less conscious of the fact that he is looking at an advertisement. Models seem to be "real" people, engaged in an earnest conversation, oblivious of the presence of the camera. An unusual touch: the woman is not smiling. Shown on the right-hand page is one of Austin Briggs's many sketches (prepared for *TV Guide*) catching people in action. Shrewd attention to detail, the mannerisms of his models, and a deliberately casual composition make Briggs's illustrations so believable that readers often forget that his drawing is not a photograph.

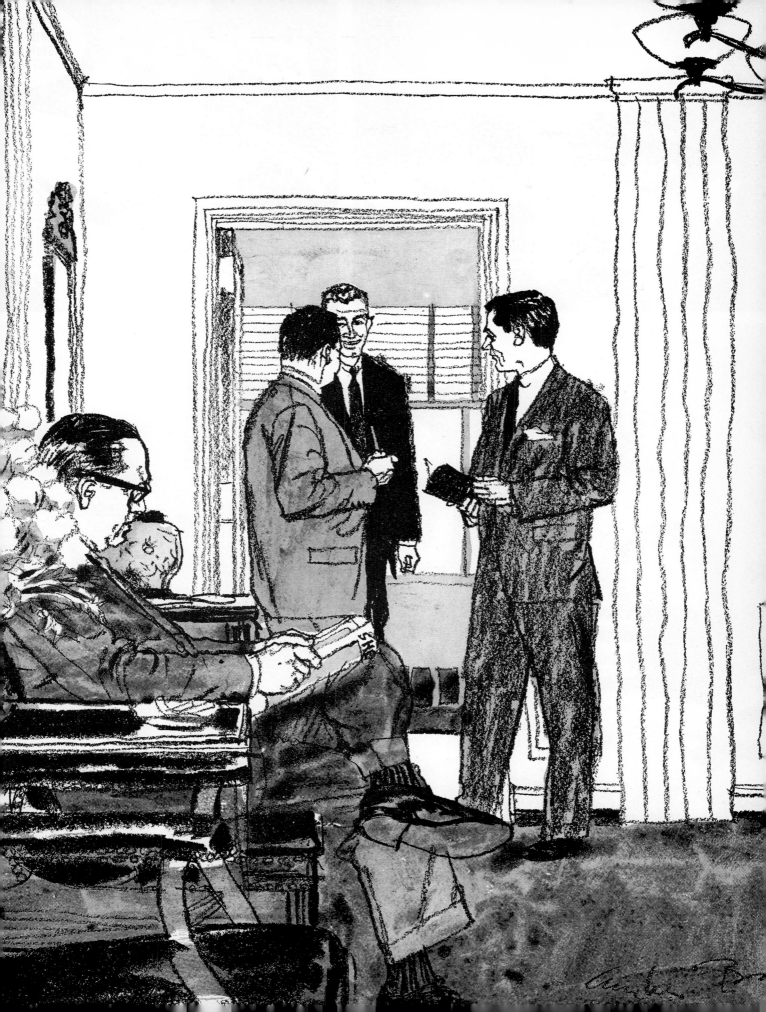

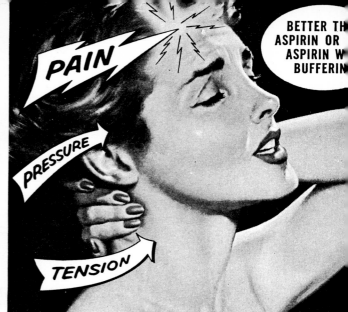

Watching the portrayal of agony in "torture commercials," advertisements for pain relievers, is not easy on the eyes. Yet these messages of doom get high attention and seem to induce people to buy the product. Why?

Every advertising agency with a drug account makes spasmodic but earnest efforts to come up with campaigns *not* featuring misery. There are some convincing arguments for eliminating the moribund people from the main illustration. As every pundit of advertising knows, readers prefer happy situations to unhappy ones. Street interviews conducted for pretesting new campaigns confirm this contention. Pictures of smiling faces usually win out over the sad ones, and the respondents make no secret of their distaste of seeing so much suffering in advertising. Still, the majority of campaigns feature pictures of men and women clutching their heads in despair.

Evidence gathered on sidewalk interviews notwithstanding, there are indications that pain-relief advertising does better with negative illustrations; people with aches apparently like to look at others writhing in pain. Personal involvement is very great here. When one major advertiser tried to run ads showing the way people feel *after* taking their pills ("Here's how . . . aspirin helps millions feel better!"), readership dropped to about one-third of that of an ad showing a contorted face. These are results of readership studies, not pretesting interviews where people tend to react to ads in a more rational (and more socially acceptable) manner.

The delectability of suffering

Headaches and muscular and other assorted aches often originate in the mind. This does not mean that these "imaginary" illnesses cause no pain to the sufferer. They do. But the uncertainty of their origin makes an accurate diagnosis extremely difficult. Thus the poor patient is not only left ailing but is also left uninformed as to the cause of his troubles. This condition will often place him in a fundamentally hostile environment. Not even his best friends seem to sympathize or believe that he has a headache. For this

reason, he unconsciously welcomes pictures of others in a similar predicament. At last he is not alone with his suffering. The more miserable the model looks in the advertisement, the more reassured he is that his pains, too, are "real."

Pictures of smiling faces bewilder the sufferer. He does not associate pleasure with pain. Contented people who have found relief hold out the possibility that his pains also can be easily remedied, that he is making a mountain out of a molehill. What he wants to see is a more credible situation (demonstration of excruciating pain), not pictures that seem, in a way, to be reproaching him for feeling sick.

The sufferer also desperately wants to know the *reasons* for his pains, so that he can explain them to himself and others. Some of the most successful pill-selling television commercials were those that spelled out, in as much detail as possible within a minute, the causes for headaches. The listing of "tension-building" factors—scenes of kids playing Indians, heavy traffic, burned meals—hit home with a large segment of the audience. Many women actually called their husbands' attention to these commercials.

The men in white coats

Few professionals receive the same degree of respect as doctors. Vance Packard, in *The Status Seekers,* found these doctors on top of the "prestige list."

There are rational reasons for this attitude. It takes many years of conscientious studying to become a doctor. The work is hard, and it is important. Also present are psychological factors. Doctors fulfill an important emotional need, especially for the pain-prone individual. He becomes an authority figure who seldom does wrong. Said Berton Roueche in his penetrating article on the use of the placebo (a medicine merely given to satisfy the patient) which appeared in *The New Yorker:* "A placebo administered in a hospital, where the patient lies surrounded by symbols of authority and care, is more likely to have an effect than one taken by someone at home."

It is safe to say that the best pill salesmen are the doctors. This is why the white-coat uniform has been so popular in television commercials for so many years. Notwithstanding the caliber of

men wearing the white jackets, these commercials have been singularly effective.

Pill buyers are interested in pictures that provide them with medical information.

Because of the earnest desire of these sufferers to prove that there are sound, hospital-tested reasons for their troubles, they welcome charts and simplified anatomical drawings.

For this reason, Bufferin's "mechanical man" (inspired by an old German drawing of the human anatomy) was an instant hit among the tablet swallowers. Here are some of the comments gathered by the interviewers of Young & Rubicam, Bufferin's agency:

"Shows just where the medicine goes in order to relieve pain."

"I think it makes the whole thing very clear."

"The ad is very informative. Sure goes into detail."

"Helps me to understand the human body."

"The drawing shows what goes on inside your body. I think that's very interesting."

"It's an unusual ad. Shows me just what happens."

Those worried about their health apparently identified themselves closely with the "mechanical man." They felt that the body shown was their own. And they were grateful for the source of material that helped them document their cases and show the world (especially their loved ones) that there were, after all, complicated reasons for their pains.

The advertiser must make sure, however, that descriptions of the gruesome details are not carried out in too much detail. Photographs like the X-ray film shown on the opposite page get close clinical scrutiny from an ailing audience but not emotional involvement. Most psychosomatic sufferers [and authorities like Dr. Harold Wolff, professor of medicine [neurology] and associate professor of psychiatry at Cornell University Medical College, estimate that 97 per cent of all headache complainers belong in this category] want to know what ails them, but only *within* reason.

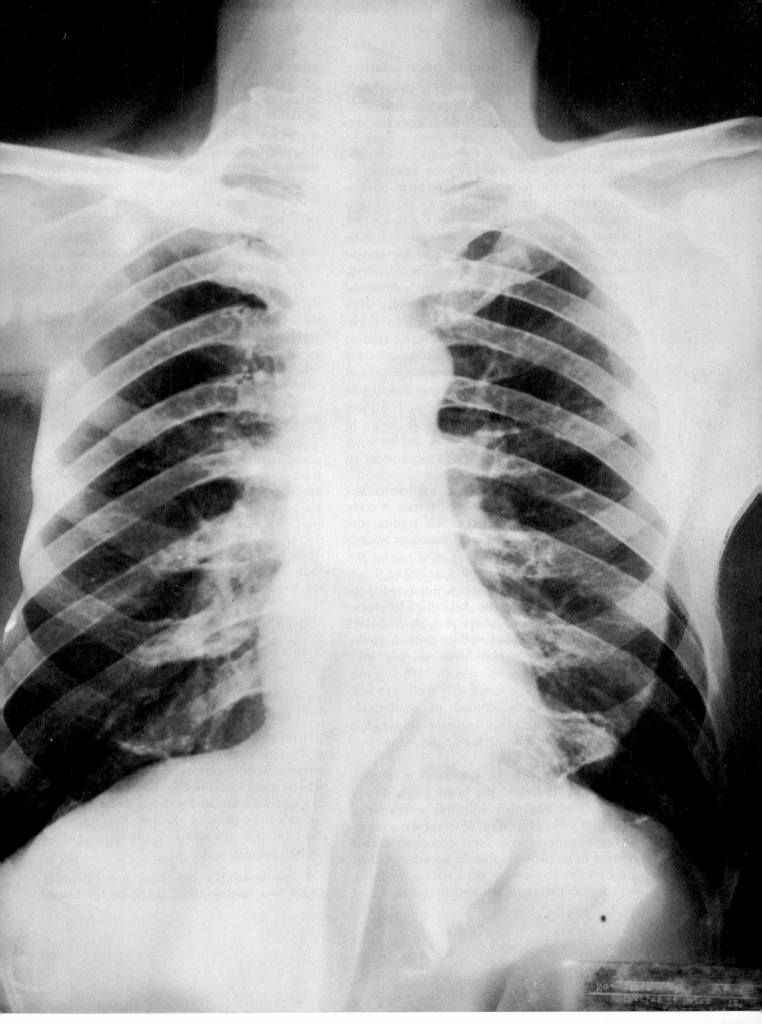

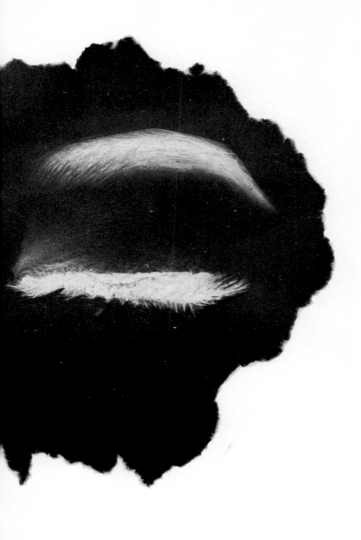

7

The mysterious minds of women

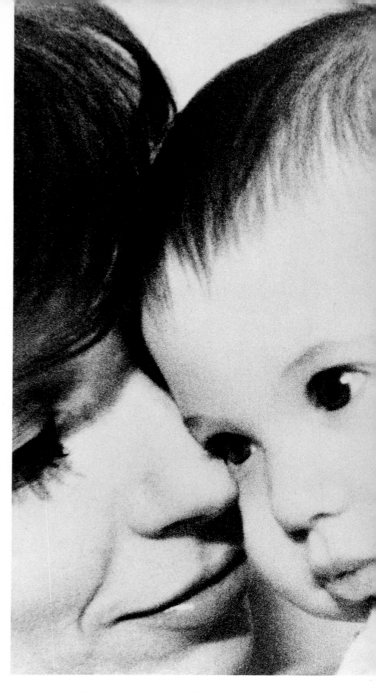

Women not only look different from men, they think and react differently.

It is important to realize what makes women buy. Their purchasing power has increased tremendously in the last few decades. So has their decision-making power. Their influence is shown in just about every product on the market, even such traditionally man-purchased items as automobiles, houses, boats, and neckties. An advertiser can no longer ignore them.

This chapter, therefore, attempts to deal with that curious being: the woman.

Women are emotionally involved with child raising. Any picture that features a baby will be noted by a large segment of women viewers, and even if they fail to remember the product advertised, they will not forget the little one pictured in the ad. Mothers like to make comparisons between their own children and those of others. Generally, women like to think of bringing up children as "fun," but realistically this is not quite so. Child raising is accompanied by a great many mundane chores. Mothers are often subconsciously torn between loving and rejecting their children. The thought of rejection is followed by strong guilt feelings. Therefore, pictures that show her actively—and pleasurably—engaged in motherhood (playing with the baby, feeding him, etc.) are usually well received. Women like to think of themselves as capable parents.

Taking care of the home—interior decorating—is a woman's prerogative. She takes great pride in her skill in furnishing a room. The home serves for her, more than for her husband, as one of the most important status symbols. She wants to impress not only her husband but her neighbors, friends, and mother-in-law as well. Because there is so much at stake emotionally, the act of home decoration is accompanied by a great deal of anxiety, much of which the woman does not even realize herself. She is acutely afraid of not living up to expectation in matters of taste. Therefore she is anxious to gather information and rely on suggestions from authorities in making purchases for the home. Pictures of model rooms will get close scrutiny from a detail-conscious woman.

A woman closely associates cooking with her ability in taking care of the family. Preparation of a meal is one of her most important—and easily available—means of receiving approval from her husband, children, and friends. She is extremely sensitive, more than she cares to admit, about her culinary skills. Failure in preparing a dish often brings up unpleasant thoughts concerning her ability to fulfill the role of a wife. She likes to see advertising that will show ways to refine some of her recipes. She welcomes ideas that make her day in the kitchen more bearable. But she resents any inferences made concerning the fact that too much reliance is being placed today on push-button methods. This suggestion makes her feel that perhaps she is failing in her duty as a home-maker.

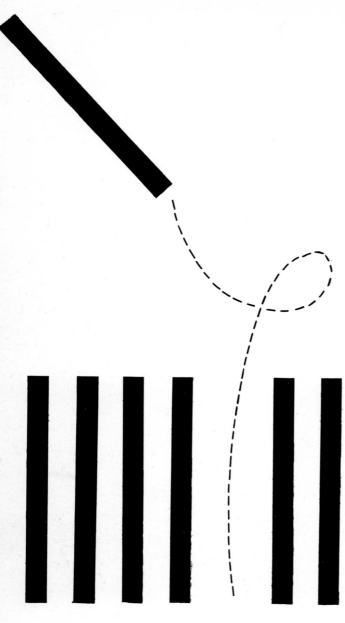

Few women are entirely satisfied with their lot in life. There is less and less prestige attached to being a housewife. In many ways women feel that their husbands are getting the better deal. They maintain that day-to-day housework is more routine than working in an office. Their arguments to back up this theory go something like this: He is exposed to new people—she is not; his work is rewarded by monetary means (and promotions)—hers is not; his environment is more stimulating. For these reasons women are in constant search for something *new*. They tend to daydream. Most of all, consciously or subconsciously, women would like to find ways to escape. Therefore pictures that promise means of "getting away from it all" usually score high in getting women's attention.

Fashion plays an important role in the life of a woman; it provides her with means to become a new person. Overtly, women often complain they are in the clutches of the clothes manufacturers who make last year's dress obsolete for economic reasons. There are indications that this kind of excuse is only a cover-up for a basic feminine urge that brings the clothing industry nearly 30 billion dollars a year. To a woman, fashion means adventure. In the last 25 years female buyers have willingly accepted such major innovations in fashion as fedora hats, ballet slippers, "The New Look," chemise, trapeze, bubble dress, low waist, high waist, and the culotte.

Romance—or thoughts of romance—offers one of the most luxurious escape mechanisms to women. They make use of it to its fullest advantage. Romantic fiction, biographies, historical novels, love stories are avidly studied by female readers. Soap operas cater almost exclusively to the frustrated housewife. It hardly matters how realistically the boy-gets-girl situations are described; women dote on them anyway. As a matter of fact, an overdose of realism may strike them as too close for comfort. Fiction stories in magazines get higher readership if illustrated not by a photographer but rather by a technically less limited artist. Identification with the heroine is always there, be it a sweet young thing, an understanding wife, or a scheming vampire.

Travel, too, offers an opportunity for a change of scenery. The fact that more and more women are taking trips (they are thought to comprise 50 to 80 per cent of the packaged trip and tour business) is interesting because the idea of making a journey is against basic feminine desires. The discomforts of travel, the lack of security (what will tomorrow bring?), temper their urge to enter into this kind of adventure. But improved accommodations and, most of all, attractive travel advertising are changing these feelings. The romantic promise of seeing new lands beckons women. They are keenly interested in meeting new people, becoming "cultured" (keeping up with the Joneses on an intellectual level), bringing home assorted items they have bought (at bargain prices) in faraway countries, and feeling young again.

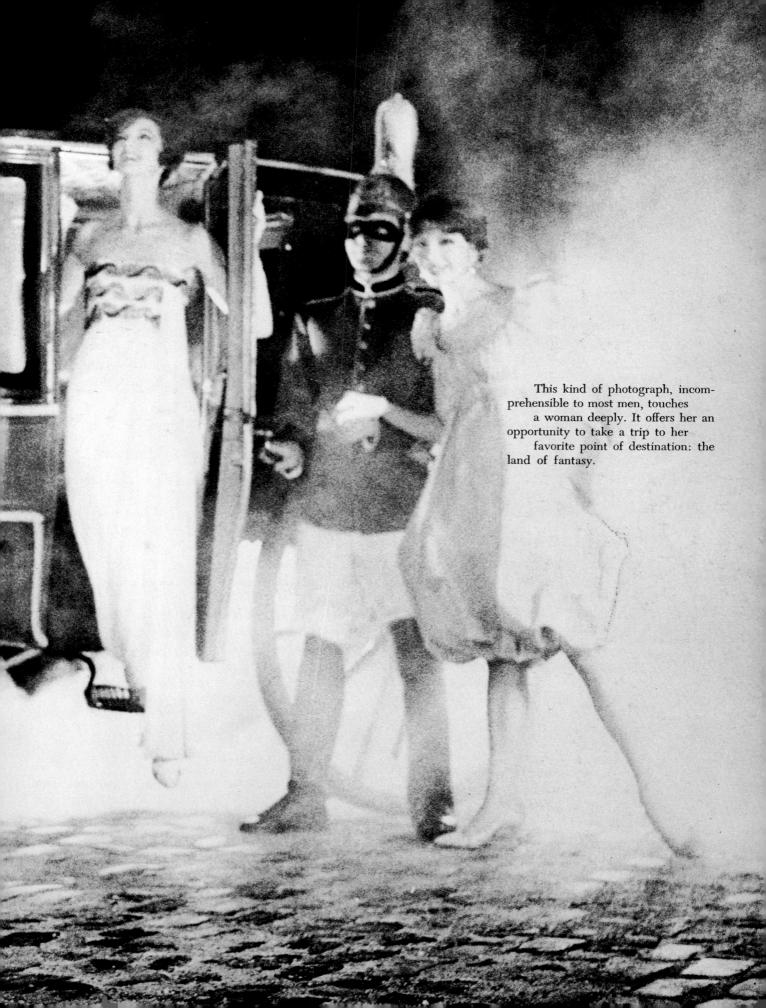

This kind of photograph, incomprehensible to most men, touches a woman deeply. It offers her an opportunity to take a trip to her favorite point of destination: the land of fantasy.

Faster than ever before in the history of mankind, the role of women is changing. The United States leads the way.

Women are not what they used to be. In the last half century they have succeeded in changing their status quo. With economic and sociological transformations came important psychological developments—as is bound to happen. These fluctuations have an important effect on modern advertising. Smart is the manufacturer who keeps ahead of the unpredictable moods of women.

Who is boss at home?

Men still bring home the bacon, but it's the women who tell them what to do with it. More women than men handle money matters at home. It is realistically impossible for the male to remain in full-time charge of family affairs; he simply doesn't have the time. Suburban living cuts into his spare hours severely. He is home only on week ends. During the week, it is the wife who makes the decisions, small and large. By default, she is assuming the household responsibilities.

Not so dumb any more.

Today women are better educated. As a result, they are more apt to feel that they are their husbands' intellectual equal. Significantly, men seem to grow increasingly tolerant of intelligent women; the majority of bachelors (55 per cent) interviewed in a poll said they preferred wives with successful business experience. Women buy books, go to concerts, and encourage their husbands to share in cultural experiences.

Freedom—it's wonderful!

With economic independence (and the knowledge that they can get a job when and if they wish to do so), a more sound educational background, and voting power that equals (and surpasses in number) that of men, women are beginning to feel more secure in their rights. They feel less dependent upon their husbands. This independence may be a contributory factor to the high divorce rates and the remarkable fact

that over 90 per cent of the cases are settled without alimony demands on the part of the interested parties.

Increased freedom has brought a new sense of importance to women. They are becoming aware of their high status and intend to keep it. Perhaps nowhere else in the world is there as much chauvinistic feeling about being a woman as in this country.

More women are better-looking.

Women are not only becoming taller (the average shoe size has jumped from 4½ to 8 in the last few decades) and healthier, but they are also finding increasing opportunities to improve their appearance. There are diets to suit every taste. Magazines with circulations in the multimillions offer beauty hints to the tune of 5 billion dollars a year.

"Let's get married—right now!"

Brides are getting younger. Marriage is met with less apprehension. Several factors are responsible for this trend. Prosperity is one; the future of the couple holds fewer financial difficulties. More enlightened sexual education, the premarital experiences of both parties, and less parental interference are other important considerations.

Young marriages encourage large families; there are more children per family today than ever before. And the boys and girls are entering adulthood before their parents reach middle age. Many modern couples find themselves grandparents while still young and vigorous.

Who lives longer?

In spite of the fact that about 5 per cent more boys than girls are born, the latter outnumber the men. The weaker sex is rapidly becoming the stronger of the two. Women are more aware of this fact than men. They no longer picture themselves as fragile, delicate creatures. And recent medical reports prove they have concrete reasons for this change in self-image.

Toreador pants and gals with slender, bony figures get raised eyebrows even from some members of their own sex. There are indications that ladies from Midwestern and Southern states—the "Bible belt"—still prefer skirts to trousers and rounder, more "feminine" figures to the elongated human fire hydrants.

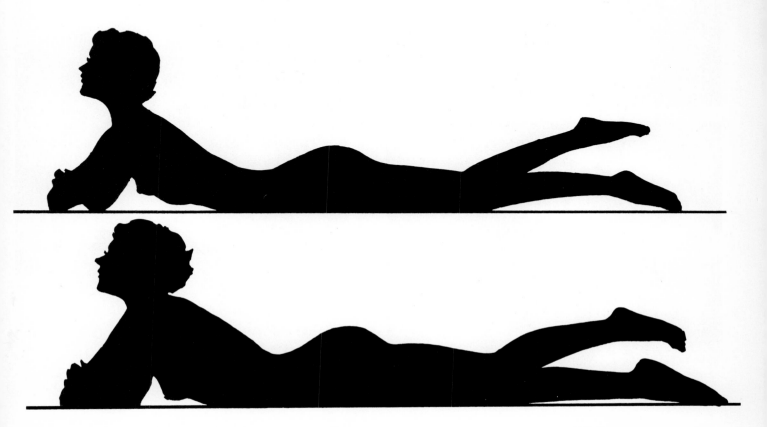

"Togetherness" was invented by a woman's magazine chiefly to please women.

Keeping up with the growing trend in family living—husband's best pal is his wife and vice versa—*McCall's* initiated the idea of "togetherness" a few years ago. Instantly advertisers took heed. Men in aprons appeared in illustrations with increased frequency. Soon he was feeding the baby, hanging up the wash, and preparing the meals. The husky husband in front of the kitchen sink (while the wife lolled in his easy chair in the living room) became a standard joke that was supposed to make both men and women smirk with delight.

"Togetherness," of course, is here to stay. Help is getting so expensive that often the husband becomes the only means of getting things done.

But there is a limit to his endurance. Psychologically, the average male is not prepared to tend a home full time. Pictures that show the male absorbed in chores that came into being only after the wedding have just a limited appeal. The idea that a husband's only source of pleasure is being with his wife has little basis in fact. Few male readers want to identify themselves with an overly domesticated husband in an illustration.

Do women like the idea?

They may think that it would be a fine thing to have such a man around the house, but instinctively women still prefer to be married to someone who knows the meaning of and how to say, "No, dear."

Today, many women are confused about their own role in life. They like to be their husbands' companions and have fun "together." On the other hand, they still feel that for a woman it is better to be dominated than to dominate. Her emotional relationship with a man must be handled more delicately than ever before.

The three pictures on this page show how versions of the same theme—romantic involvement between man and woman—can be handled. The photograph on top gets higher female self-identification than the picture on the bottom.

I am adaptable, aesthetic, attractive, capricious, charming, cooperative, cunning, emotional, heedful, intuitive, kind, loyal, money-wise, motherly, mysterious, not-easy-to-fool, practical, precious, sensitive, smart, sociable, style-conscious, vivacious, wise, wonderful. I am a woman!

A woman's sense of humor is different from a man's. Photograph on this page is well executed but teases women unmercifully; the message is delivered too bluntly. The whimsical illustration of a girl wearing froth instead of a hat (used in a Prell advertisement), on next page, is the type of whimsy women enjoy. The joke is more refined and presented in good taste; this is woman-to-woman talk, which a whopping 80 per cent of all female readers of the magazine recalled a month after its publication.

In cosmetics pictures, the ones showing the finished results are more effective than those demonstrating the application of the stuff. Women apparently believe that applying cosmetics is an involved and rather tiresome task; the fun starts *after* the process is completed.

Curiously enough, little of this feeling exists in the case of soap advertising. A picture of a model with her face or hands enveloped in foam receives favorable acceptance among women. Washing is an act closely associated with purification; even in her younger days she was encouraged by her parents to wash up. The use of cosmetics, on the other hand, may still be accompanied (especially among the less sophisticated) with recollections of parental disapproval.

Women prefer to be told about problems of personal hygiene on a formalized, impersonal level. They do *not* want to be identified with the model and would rather think of her as a demonstrator of the product. The photograph of the back view of a woman shown on this page sold the merchandise hard, whereas a competitive brand's illustration of a woman engaged essentially in the same activity but *facing* her audience did poorly on noting and reading. Shown on the right-hand page is a highly effective television commercial devised for Ban deodorant. The scenes are documentary, realistically fast-moving, yet the subject of using the product is handled with shrewd delicacy.

Ban takes the
worry out of
being close

Most men find the picture on the left amusing. But it makes a great many women feel uncomfortable. They do not like to mix humor with sex. The sketchy rendition of a nude on this page (used in a full-page ad for Franklin Simon department store) gets collective nods from female readers; the arty technique softens impact of nudity. Anyway, the heroine is "someone else."

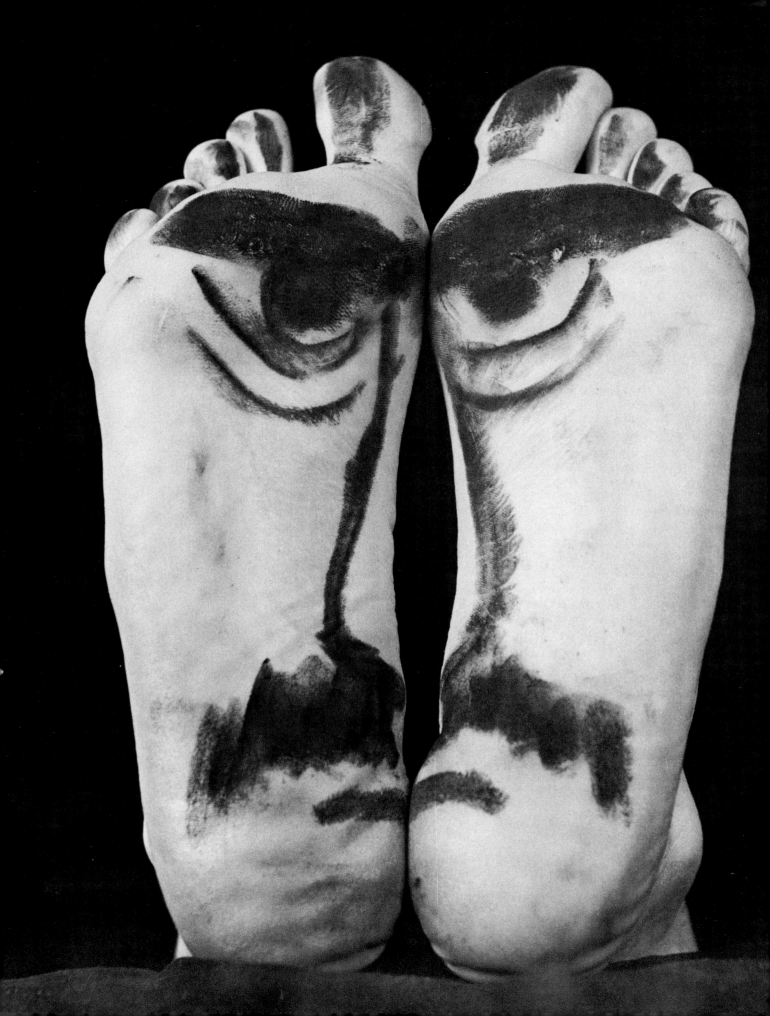

You'll be head-over-heels in love with the new fun shades by Cutex. Which to try first? You'll run out of fingers and toes before you decide! Because Cutex has lots of gay new polish colors you've never worn before. And Summer is the time to try them. The time to experiment with mad, marvelous shades like "Coral Sand" and "Capri Blue." The time to tip your toes with Pearls and be a lovely sea siren. You're not in the fashion swim until you try Cutex fun shades.

FUN SHADES
all the summery
Pearl Polishes by
CUTEX

Grotesqueness must be combined with beauty in order to make it acceptable to the female beholder. Photograph of feet with face painted on them is a brutal, direct presentation of an entertaining idea. Men rarely object to such a picture. In the advertisement above, the exaggerated pose is shocking to the eye, but the photograph's inherent beauty (girl is displaying range of nail-polish colors) and gentle humor get knowing smiles from women.

A woman is highly sensitive about her appearance. Indiscriminate cropping of her face usually lowers readership. Many a poster has lost part of its potential female audience for this reason. Men couldn't care less about their faces being cut in half.

These advertising approaches are psychologically sound. Women accept them, understand them, and act upon them:

This advertisement features a woman perching comfortably on a goal pedestal. She is dressed in a pleated tunic top and sleek red trousers (explains text: "Rogers places you there with equal parts of school girl and siren"), and her pose is highly seductive indeed. The man leaning against the pedestal appears to be the proud possessor. The relationship suggested here appeals to both male and female readers. She is being cherished by her husband (or lover), and in a subtle way she exercises control over him. But it is her delectable charm, *not* overt domination, that keeps him from running away. The situation does not keep her from feeling feminine nor him from being aware of his masculine prerogatives.

Have you just about had it?

Are your spirits sagging? Give yourself a lift. Shop where you find the world's best cheerer-uppers: beautiful fashions...at prices so low, you'll be amazed at how little it will take to make you happy. Next time things look bleak (and even if they don't!) come in to the store that's a real cheerer-upper, Ohrbach's.

Remember how great cigarettes used to taste?
LUCKIES STILL DO

CHANGE TO LUCKIES
and get some taste for a change!

Shrewd psychological insight makes this Ohrbach advertisement a powerful invitation for women to come to the store. The main illustration features a girl leaning on a mop for obvious reasons. Beckons headline: "Have you just about had it?" Copy goes on to suggest that you "give yourself a lift . . . you'll be amazed how little it will take to make you happy." The creator of this advertisement knew that the idea of shopping "downtown" (Ohrbach's is midtown, but what does it matter?) serves as an emotional outlet for a woman. With the adventure of shopping goes a pleasant, tingling anticipation of something "new" and, most of all, a break in the day-to-day routine of taking care of a home.

The kind of "togetherness" that is readily acceptable to both sexes is displayed in this advertisement for Lucky Strike. The girl in the picture is not a prototype of glamour, but she is exceedingly pretty—the kind of woman that is liked by both male and female friends. She seems to be the "outdoor type." There is strong emotional involvement with the situation here. This is a young couple living in a home; they are scanning through their morning mail. There is a suggestion that their relationship is based on mutual understanding. The picture exudes warmth, companionship, and, most of all, a happy home life. Just as getting a man is an important activity in the life of a woman, so is keeping him. This ad reassures her of success in the latter.

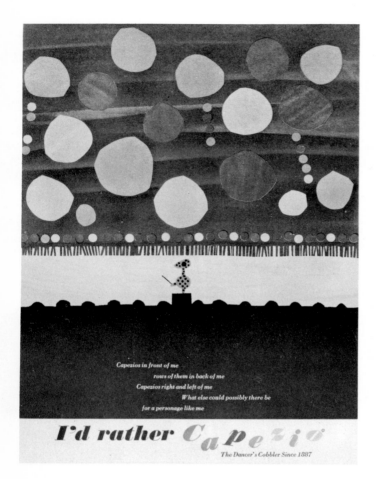

Capezios in front of me
rows of them in back of me
Capezios right and left of me
What else could possibly there be
for a personage like me

I'd rather Capezio

The Dancer's Cobbler Since 1887

Your new, fair world *bright with a diamond's li...*

Sharing a love, sharing carefree, dream-lit days, you find a new, fair world that's yours a... when you're engaged. And the promise that has wrought this lovely miracle is told in your en... ment diamond. This light of lights was born of earth to shine for you through time and cha... through happiness and tears, your testament of love unending. Your ring-stone may be me... in size, but should be chosen with care, for it will be treasured by you and generations yet t...

HOW TO BUY A DIAMOND First, and most important, consult a trusted jeweler. Ask about color, clarity and cutting—for these determine a diamond's quality, contribute to its beauty and value. Choose a fine stone, and you'll always be proud of it, no matter what its size. Diamond sizes are measured by weight, in points and carats—100 points to the carat. (Exact weights shown are seldom found.) For your guidance, the price ranges given above are based on current quotations by jewelers throughout the country in July, 1960. Note that prices vary widely according to the qualities offered. Tax is additional.

A diamond is foreve...

Gay, colorful painting of a spotted little "personage" leading an orchestra in front of a polka-dotted curtain is the kind of utterly silly whimsy that leaves men befuddled and women enchanted. It takes reading the text to discover the merchandise being sold here (shoes). This is subtle salesmanship that works through suggestion of mood rather than matter-of-fact explanation of the subject. Women are keenly receptive to this kind of persuasion. They appreciate the beauty of the illustration. They also perceive the frivolous sophistication of the designer in using this type of art work. Consequently they feel they are being "talked up" to; this makes them feel that they are smart and knowing and possess good taste.

The campaign sponsored by the De Beers Company has been appearing for many years. It did for diamonds what Steuben has done for glassware. The precious stone became a symbol of enduring love. Art work—as in the ad shown above—is always elegant, formal, and beautiful. Since women have important influence on purchases of wedding rings, the pictures suggest romance. Men look at these ads, but female readership outranks that of male. This kind of ethereal treatment of a subject falls neatly in with her dreams. It takes sex out of love and courtship and puts romance back into it—to the delight of women and the possible dismay of men. It makes the subject of buying a ring appear to be not just a commercial transaction but rather an act of devotion.

Courtesy of
Procter & Gamble

Mr. Clean—the friendly genie symbolizing the power of a washing detergent—became an instant hit among housewives. The psychological reasons for his love affair with Mrs. America are revealing. In bleaches—as in men—she wants *strength* (Chlorodine had little trouble establishing itself). Mr. Clean is bursting with latent power. Facing her weekly wash load, a woman subconsciously longs for male help. Mr. Clean is the milkman, postman, plumber, and Lady Chatterley's lover all rolled into one. He is ready to assist, sympathetic to her needs, and familiar with the mechanics of the washing machine. While the husband is always gallivanting in the office ("He has it easy"), Mr. Clean is pinch-hitting for him at home.

This travel advertisement for Nassau and the Bahamas reaches many a potential woman customer. It points to an important reason for her taking the trip—the possibility of buying merchandise she could not get at home. Women like to bring back mementos of their excursions into foreign lands. Shopping in a native straw market in Nassau can be even more exciting than a crowded downtown department store. There is an opportunity to use her clever bargaining powers to their fullest advantage. Most of all, she will be able to show her newly acquired goodies to all her friends who did not have the luck of being able to stray so far away from home. All her purchases will serve as conversation pieces in living-room tête à têtes on travel adventures.

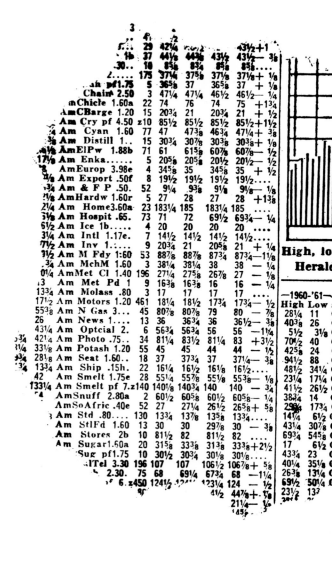

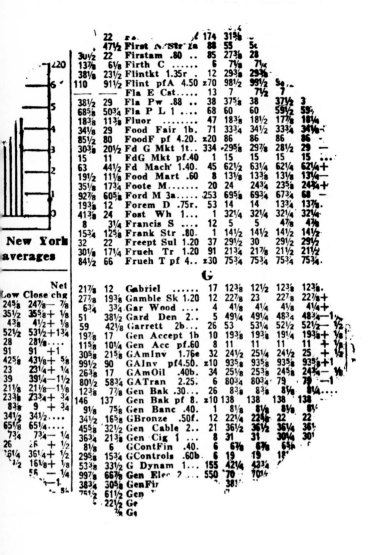

8

The art of building a corporate image

What is your "corporate image"? Presented here are a few possible definitions. Pick the one that you feel suits your company best.

If you find that your company meets the particulars of three or four (or more) portrayals here, look out. You may be part of an organization that has a diffused, "smorgasbord" image.

?

"Personality" of the company	*vernacular definition*
modern	"Those fellows are ahead of the time They are always working on this or tha something we'll be able to use in the futur They have spent a lot of money on research Everything they do has a sort of modern up-to-date look to it."
conservative	"Good, steady bunch of people. You ca always depend on them; they'll be in busi ness for a long time. As my father used t say, 'Such companies are the mainstay o American business. Others come and go and create depression times, but not *this* com pany.'"
friendly	"Nice people. I wouldn't mind havin some of those guys up to my house for beer. They are really interested in you, and they know your problems. Bet they hav good pension plans. None of their bosses ar stuck-up, if you know what I mean."
mighty	"A very large company—so big that I don' think most people in it know each other They've got millions of dollars in the kitty Everybody gets steady raises. Do a lot of work for the government; they're the only ones who can do those big jobs. Oh boy imagine the money they make!"
sophisticated	"They live in a world of their own which is out of my league, but I guess it's all right for some people. They do nice work, if you like that sort of thing. Pretty sure, their offices must be in some big metropolitan city like New York. My wife appreciates their stuff more than I do."

You cannot present one face to the stockholders ("We are a conservative group"), another to salesmen ("Our people are real go-getters"), and still another to the general public ("We are a large organization yet small, sophisticated yet down-to-earth, clever manipulators but plain folk at heart") and still hope to emanate a clear, easy-to-understand image to those with whom you come in contact.

advantages	disadvantages	yes	no
e public expects a company to put new oducts on the market and will take them their confidence quickly. It looks toward management for leadership. Feelings of ro-worship are present here. (Example: M)	Some people tend to believe that a company is risking its stockholders' money on blue-sky adventures; cost of unrealized ambitions is passed on to the customer. The majority of the American public begrudgingly respects those seeking change but feels uncomfortable when status quo is challenged.	☐	☐
is type of company attracts investors who e interested in gradual but sure capital preciation. Men from other conservative rporations have especially kindred feel-gs toward this company and like to take eir business here. (Example: Metropolitan fe Insurance)	Missing is the essential ingredient of youthful zest, so much a part of the American folklore. The company is sometimes associated with the old-time evils of being too large and rich, exploiting its workers. It is apt to be suspected of one-sided political affiliations, i.e., Republican.	☐	☐
ople have trust in the company, in their llingness to act on complaints. There is e belief that the company considers the easing of its customers of primary importance. There are likely to be warm, personal feelings toward members of corporation. (Example: management of the American Baseball League)	There may be the impression that many employees of the corporation are not professionally as capable as they should be but obtained their positions through social contacts. Not consistent with the image is the ruthless, dynamic figure of a man who "gets things done"; a void that the public often associates with lack of efficiency.	☐	☐
arge companies are strongly associated th efficiency. They use the latest methods, e best machines, and employ top talent. ey offer an important measure of security time of war. The public knows they e rich but resents this fact less than they uld have in the past. (Example: Du Pont)	Being rich is no longer a crime, but there still prevails some antagonism toward those in a position to change one's fate. Individual reactions to giant companies vary with subjective attitudes toward authority figures. Those looking for father substitutes often find their emotional needs fulfilled through association with these corporations.	☐	☐
ompanies surrounded with an aura of phistication are taste-makers. They are oked upon as pioneers in matters of aesetics. Rarely does the average man or oman feel qualified enough to pass judgent on the innovations coming from these ganizations. (Example: Herman Miller ssociates)	Unappreciative of the esoteric ingredients of the merchandise, people often label such companies clearing houses for the "phonies." They are accused of losing touch—at their own choosing—with the "common people" and letting artistic considerations overpower the practical ones.	☐	☐

"Personality" of the company	*vernacular definition*
down-to-earth	"I like them because when they do some thing, they do it. There is no nonsense abo this company. It is run by people like yo and me. They're in business to make mone but they give you good service. Yes, that what they are: good, solid, hard-hittir business people."
masculine	"The company is run by *men*. You ca tell just by watching them. They work har nights if they have to. There just isn't ar place for a woman there. Their product a man's product, too. I don't think a woma ever uses it, or at least she never real thinks about it."
feminine	(*from a woman*) "They know my prob lems. When it comes to nice things, the sure have good taste. They're always com ing up with new items. I don't know hov they get their ideas, but they do. A woma next door told me about their product, ar after I used it, I told my best friend abou it."
manufacturer	"These guys *make* things, not sell then They have the best people working for then —I don't mean salesmen and advertisin men, I mean scientists, technicians, machin ists. They know what they are doing or els they wouldn't be in business."
salesman	"They do anything to sell me on thei services. Really cooperative people, though I have nothing against them, except they ar trying to make me buy something, and don't like that. Yet they are always tryin to improve their services (or product), an certainly I appreciate their efforts."
idealistic	"The people working for this compan have big ideas. I know, I've read a speec their president made the other day. H wasn't talking about his company at all; h was giving those guys in Washington blast. A real American."
pragmatic	"No fooling around here. These guy know what they want. They're all busines Everything is figured out on a practica basis."

advantages	disadvantages	yes	no
...e average person feels hardy sympathy ...th these companies; often he would like ...actively participate in their business ad-...ntures. The alleged toughness on the part ...management neatly fits into the Ameri-...n stereotyped conception of business lead-...ship. (Example: International Harvester)	To those endowed with more sensitive personalities, the policies of such corporations seem a little too direct, unsubtle. Brute strength inherent in these organizations makes the more intellectually inclined feel unwelcomed.	☐	☐
...eople believe that the company takes a ...usinesslike approach to its problems, and ...there are any flaws in its operational pro-...edure, they are quickly rectified by man-...gement. Both men and women assume ...plicitly that the world of business belongs ...the male. (Example: Standard Oil)	There are few disadvantages to a company's having a "masculine" image unless it is engaged in manufacturing a woman's product. Then there might be a slight possibility that *some* women would feel their problems were not understood.	☐	☐
...o get a woman's confidence it is important ...at she feel in rapport with the company ...nd believe that they are aware of her ...ighly specialized needs. She associates ..."femininity" with smartness, a keener, more ...ensitive insight into the "finer things in ...fe." (Example: Elizabeth Arden)	Curiously enough, even women want to see the presence of *some* male leadership in a company. They assume that some day, somehow, a situation will arise in the organization that will overwhelm the females—such as a leaking roof. They are not quite sure if the company is capable of surviving crises.	☐	☐
...eople feel that the company is a specialist ...its field of endeavor and that its energies ...re channeled in a single direction. Special-...zed technical know-how has always been ...highly respected attribute in this country. ...uch companies, in the minds of the public, ...re highly dependable. (Example: Fairchild ...viation)	There is lack of close, personal feeling toward the company. The tendency is to associate such an organization with facts and figures; what they do may be more impressive than what they are. Going about its task with relentless determination, the company is often compared to a giant austere piece of machinery.	☐	☐
...With the consumer put in the driver's seat, ...here is a pleasant realization that his inter-...sts are being seriously considered. The ...dea that the company is acting as a sales-...man subconsciously makes the customer feel ...uperior to the company, giving him certain ...eal—and imaginary—rights. (Example: Hil-...on Hotels)	Such organizations usually enjoy great popularity (their livelihood depends on it), but they often fail to arouse the kind of awesome respect given to their brethren in the "manufacturing business."	☐	☐
...It is assumed that mercenary considerations ...eceive no priority here. The company re-...ceives recognition not only by its leader-...ship in industry but also by its vigorous ap-...proach to economic and political affairs. It ...is apt to get particularly strong support ...from the more intellectual segment of the ...population. (Example: Bell & Howell)	The more stodgy members of the American populace distrust the motives of such corporations and are quick to tag them "radical." Points of views expressed are often resented not on the basis of content but on the fact that "these guys had better stick to their business."	☐	☐
The American culture is based on strong pragmatic beliefs. The uncomplicated aspects of such a philosophy appeal to the average man on the street; he not only understands but likes it. Therefore, he feels at home with the viewpoints of such a company. (Example: General Motors)	It is a little too simple and pat for the more complex individual. Old-time, opportunistic business methods are often thought to be an outgrowth of pragmatic tenets in this country; men in these companies are often labeled "old-timers."	☐	☐

Is the building of a "corporation image" worth all the fuss?

It is possible to prepare sound advertising and at the same time conveniently ignore the task of building a corporate image. Sometimes, immediate sales gains are more important than long-range prospects. In mail-order advertising, for example, the product usually gets more emphasis than the company who makes it—and justifiably so.

It is safe to say, however, that in the majority of cases it is good business to work toward an increase in sales *and* a development of a definite corporate image. This is true especially of those companies who hope to stay in business for a number of years. Most companies fall into this category.

The term *corporate image* has been befogged with so much mumbo jumbo that sometimes we forget just what is meant by it. There is really no mystery here. Corporate image is a person's spontaneous idea of a company. It is a composite of all the things associated with the organization and the product it fabricates.

It is not something that can be casually picked up like a suit of clothing. There are few business enterprises today without some sort of image they can claim exclusively. There are no *successful* corporations in existence without it. Even small organizations have images. The corner grocery store caters to those living in the immediate neighborhood, and its owner most likely works diligently on his image with housewives. Drugstores, too, labor on developing a personality all their own in order to become a second home to teen-agers. Even newsstands have images.

When large organizations find themselves without the benefit of clear-cut corporate images, there is usually trouble in the offing. The source of problems may be so hard to spot that the ailment defies diagnosis, and the company disappears from the economic scene without anyone's knowing the real reason why.

Case histories of defunct enterprises convincingly demonstrate the importance of easily definable images. The floundering of *Collier's* magazine started long before its final departure from the publication world; features were added and subtracted, cover designs were changed, editors were hired and fired; and yet in the end there was failure. *Collier's* had no image. Neither the public nor the advertisers knew what to make of it.

The coming and going of the Edsel car offers another dramatic example that groping for an image is not enough—one must be found before the curtains fall. This automobile received the support of one of the largest and most experienced companies in the world. Little was left to conjecture. Many millions of dollars were poured into advertising and promotion. Somewhere along the line the car was even given a "personality" (for those "on their way up"), but this was never systematically followed through. The public could never quite fit Edsel into its dream. Was it a car for the rich or poor, the young or old, the highbrow or lowbrow, the adventurous or the conservative? The name suggested nothing. Neither did the design. Promotional efforts were diffused. Edsel had to be taken off the market three years and 400 million dollars later.

Even an industry—the complete category—faces problems when it finds its image is unclear. Wall Street had its share of woes in the past when the rich were really rich and the poor were really poor. More recently, the advertising industry, "Madison Avenue," has been pounced upon by the general populace. Ironically enough, the disagreement among advertising pundits themselves as to the purpose of their being and their lack of confidence in their usefulness are the primary causes for the confused image here. On one extreme are those who maintain that the advertising man is the savior of the American economy and without him there would be an imminent collapse of all that is good. At the other extreme are the cynics who make Madison Avenue the scapegoat for all that is evil. The public is not quite sure whom to believe, and in the meantime industry suffers.

When a nation is left without a crisp, to-the-point image, the consequences can be monumental. At the present time, the world population finds the image of the United States of America a baffling one indeed. Are we as materialistic and money-mad as Russian propagandists would like people to believe? Or are we the generous, soft-touch nation that our foreign-aid programs suggest? Democracy preaches equality of races. Yet there is wild and outspoken discrimination in this country. Our schools are great in number.

But anti-intellectualism is more rampant here than anywhere else on the globe. And so, though the United States is blessed with many assets, a clear-cut public image ("world image" would be a more appropriate term) is not one of them.

Images are not built in a day.

"Image building" requires skillful—and patient —long-term planning. The question is *not* what will the next few days bring. The aim is to create an impression of the company that will last for many years to come.

To dismiss the entire undertaking of image development with a shoulder-shrugging reaction to one or two advertisements ("Okay, run them") is naïve and silly. The fabrication of a corporate profile demands not one or two magazine insertions or a few television commercials but a sustained—and consistent—advertising program.

Neither is it realistic to hope that advertising alone will establish a fast public image for the firm. Advertising is only a single expression—an important one, to be sure—of the company's philosophy. But there are other tentacles that also reach out and touch the interested parties. The appearance of the factory buildings, the type of service the company offers its customers, the kind of speeches its officials utter, and last but not least the quality of the product the company manufactures make up the ingredients for a corporate image.

Images can be changed.

The care by which company images are built does not preclude the possibility that when and if the need arises, they can be changed. Granted, this is a chore of no small magnitude; it can be costly. But it can be done.

When the National Tea Council learned that tea had a meek, passive image ("Tired? Nervous? Try tea") and therefore only had a limited acceptance among males, it set out to change this state of affairs. Through advertising ("Drink it hefty, hot, and hearty. Take tea and see!") it succeeded. Sales went up 11 per cent in one year.

Marlboro cigarettes, too, changed their image from "feminine" to "masculine." The bold photographic close-ups of husky males, with tattoos on their hands to signify their humble beginnings, put the cigarette among the top six.

The hard-liquor industry is in the throes of making the same kind of switch—in reverse. Drinking hard liquor has always been a sign of masculinity. The introduction in advertising of delicate feminine creatures, shown sniffing the whisky glass with dignity but not without interest, is going to help this industry expand into hitherto unexplored markets.

More recently, the beer industry has been following suit in making beer a woman's drink, too. Photographs of ladies sipping a glassful have shown up in various magazines.

More and more organizations are taking a close look at their image. For some products, especially those in the package goods field, a bit of old-fashionedness is not necessarily harmful: witness the longevity of such charmers as Betty Crocker or Aunt Jemima. But for most companies a senile image can mean a slowdown in sales. Just as people, products have lives, too. When products reach maturity and adulthood, things must be done to keep them going: a new package perhaps, a new slogan, a new design, new ingredients. The American market is a highly volatile one. According to the A. C. Nielsen Company—world's largest marketing research organization—of the 100 leading brands heading their respective categories, 30 had lost their leadership after only six years, and within another five years, 30 per cent of the *new* top 30 were no longer leading the parade.

Many companies today are in the process of changing—or refining—their images. Most of them would like to be brought up to date so that the public will not think of them as being old-fashioned. Among these image-changers are such well known names as Union Carbide, General Electric, International Mining & Chemical, Torrington, Ansul, Kimberly-Clark, Ciba, National Biscuit, Upjohn, Jones & Laughlin, Johnson's Wax, West Virginia Pulp & Paper, United Airlines, and United Van Lines. Similar programs are on the drawing boards for such other large corporations as American Machine & Foundry, Trans-World Airlines, Youngstown Steel, Olin Mathieson, and Minnesota Mining & Manufacturing.

Does image building deserve all this attention? These companies—some of the most successful in America—seem to think so.

The ethereal quality of Renoir's paintings, his predilection for soft, pastel coloring, would make him a favorite with perfume advertisers.

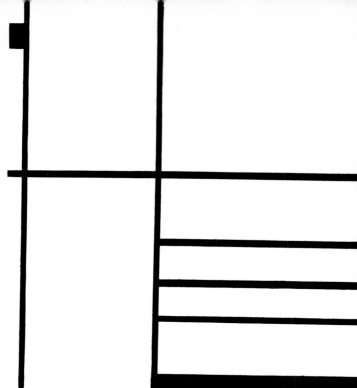

Mondrian's stark, modern technique would enable him to take charge of all graphics in a large corporation interested primarily in institutional advertising.

The classical style that gives the beholder a feeling of serenity would make Michelangelo a logical choice to illustrate bank or insurance advertisements.

Feed manufacturers, directing their sales story to farmers, would welcome Thomas Benton's bold, realistic style with undertones of "social message."

spirited yet highly controlled linear treatment so
al of Toulouse-Lautrec would command high prices
g fashion advertisers today.

ndma Moses' uncomplicated approach to life, so elo-
ntly stated in her primitive, gay-colored reminiscences,
ild serve candy manufacturers well.

Once the general concept as to the image of
a company is determined—not by a tentative
agreement between two or three executives at
a lower level but by everyone in the company
as accurately as possible—the next problem will
demand investigation: how to establish the desired image. Soon the question will arise:

Is the "visual profile"
consistent with
the over-all image of
your company?

Art work put forth by the organization has profound influence in molding public opinion about
it, much more than is often realized. Think of
it in these terms: Even the most articulate individual fails to make a good impression on his
listener if his clothes are shabby or if his appearance in any way belies his words.

On these two pages are works of classic, well-
known painters. Were they looking for commercial assignments today, they would fit neatly
into the scheme of things. Their highly individ-
ualistic style would help greatly toward the
building of corporate images.

Add to the six artists represented on these pages
the vast legion of illustrators, photographers, designers, art directors, all available these days to
tackle graphic problems, and you will realize
the potentiality of every company to create a
visual profile all its own.

When the management of Titeflex, Incorporated—a company in Springfield, Massachusetts, that manufactures flexible metal hose and accessories—decided to develop a graphic program that would reflect the progressive philosophy of the organization, they called in top designer Lester Beall. He developed five alternates for a new trade mark (including suggestions for logotype and company color scheme) from which one was chosen.

modern

A symbol, such as the one developed for Titeflex, often serves as a pacesetter. Crisp, distinctive, and modern, the Titeflex monogram lent a basic direction to all the visual expressions which subsequently emanated from the company. Few items escaped the designer's attention. His thoroughness—and insistence on the part of management that everything should have the "same look"—made this face-lifting operation particularly successful.

NEWS RELEASE

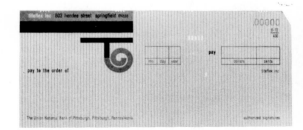

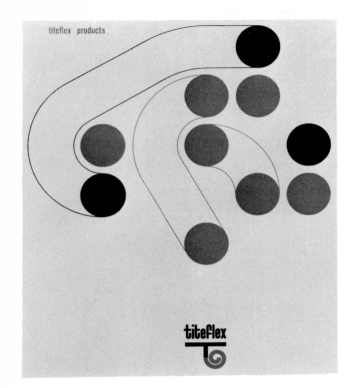

titeflex products

titeflex

flexible hose and couplings flexible hose and couplings flexible hose and couplings

titeflex inc springfield mass titeflex inc springfield mass titeflex inc springfield mass

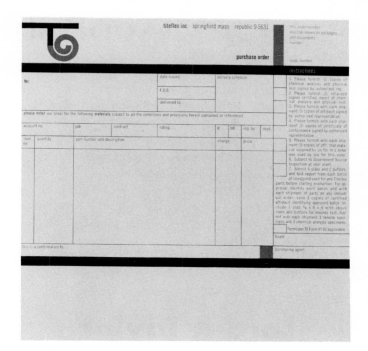

now...an old company presents a new face...an image...a dynamic trademark to match the many changes that are making Titeflex the most progressive company in the flexible hose industry...this trademark is symbolic of our faith in the future...in our employees...in the city of Springfield, where a progressive spirit exemplified by its urban renewal program is meeting the demands of modern industry

Few people realize that Lord & Taylor is almost a century and a half old. The store is associated with a great many characteristics, but antiquity isn't one of them. As a matter of fact, customers think of Lord & Taylor as a *young* establishment, full of vigor and pioneering spirit. They also like to refer to it as a "woman's store" which not only follows fashion trends but also makes them. Lord & Taylor is a place for "smart" shoppers.

The clear, vigorous image of the store did not come about by accident. Almost from the beginning it was carefully nurtured by some of the wisest merchandising minds in the country. Today, this image is maintained by consistent meth-

sophisticated

ods, scientific as well as artistic. The institution keeps a large number of top talent on staff—and they are working full time. About 25 display men make sure that the store puts up a good front. Buyers are trained to be "not only selectors but also creative developers of merchandise." Sales girls are carefully chosen. The store has a good-sized art department which keeps an art director, layout men, sign painters constantly searching for new graphic expressions. Almost all art work (exceptions are the drawings prepared for advertising) is done there. To assure the "Lord & Taylor look" in every endeavor, all creative functions are coordinated in the New York store.

Lord & Taylor   *Lord & Taylor*

First to develop a free-swinging, "informal" signature, Lord & Taylor gave its advertising a look all its own. The scribble has been in use since 1933, showing up on everything from stationary to shopping bags. Says Harry Rodman, art director of the store: "Ours is not just a set logo. It is a personalized signature that becomes an integral part of the over-all design. Like a piece of handwriting, we change it a little here, a little there, depending on its use, but you can always tell that it's Lord & Taylor's."

To attract the type of customers which the store usually compels, Lord & Taylor has set the tone for its seven branch establishments through architectural designs (the majority have been done with Raymond Loewy Associates acting as designers and planners). An attempt is made to present a graceful exterior appearance complementary to the community which surrounds it. For example, the building in Washington, D.C. (bottom photo), follows the classic mood of the city with its totally white façade and monumental tone of design.

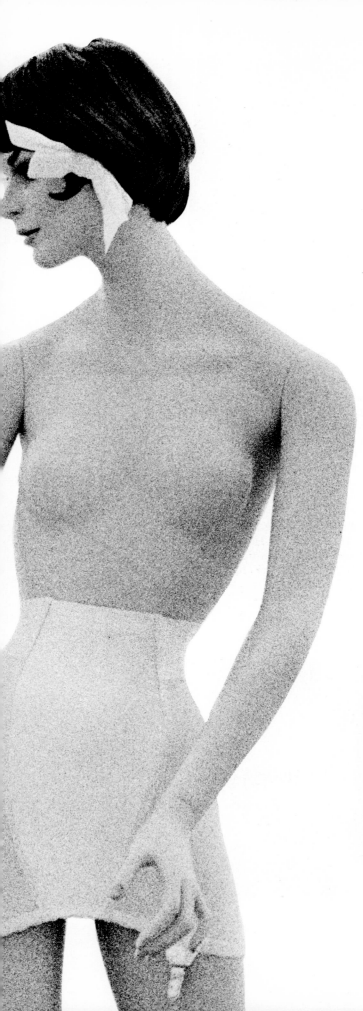

Still another part of the Lord & Taylor personality is the pacesetting windows—the first ones which could be raised or lowered to any height, so as to allow a wide range of designs. Shown on the opposite page are two of the store's famous Christmas windows that draw thousands of spectators year after year. No detail is overlooked. Even the mannequins are carefully chosen. More sophisticated than those shown in other stores (Peck & Peck likes them young and prim; Saks prefers the demure ones; and Bergdorf of course wants creatures that exude quiet richness), they are consistent with the personality of Lord & Taylor.

Close to thirty interior decorators make sure that customers get a whiff of Lord & Taylor's sophisticated air once inside. Displays are changed often. Shown on this page is an example of what happens when the store's top interior designers are turned loose. Each interior decorator had an opportunity to trim a Christmas tree in his own department. The ornamentation is widely different, but common throughout are ingenuity and good taste. On the right-hand page are Christmas cards designed by four (out of some fifteen) eminent Lord & Taylor freelance artists, Carl Wilson (working for the store for twenty-eight years), Helen Hall, Dorothy Hood, and Carol Blanchard. The store works closely with its artists and was the first client of its kind to encourage contributors to sign all advertising art work.

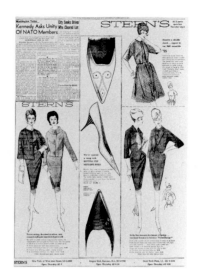

Says Melvin E. Dawley, president: "We are trying to use our advertising to announce an idea, a look, rather than give a detailed description of a specific item." The spirit of Lord & Taylor advertising is different from that of any of its competitors.

"Oh, it's a long, long time

from May to December—"

but how we love the waiting game

in Lord & Taylor's Fur Storage!

On the Tenth Floor

Call Wisconsin 7-3300 for

cleaning and storage service

Every year, as in most large department stores, promotions are staged to build traffic. Lord & Taylor uses a graphic theme for almost all its promotional campaigns. The rose shown above symbolizes the coming of spring and, incidentally, a fashion trend (said advertising copy: "There are ravishing rose blossoms on evening gowns, lingerie, linens—rose-colored coats and suits and dresses and shoes—rose-tinted make-up, fragrant rose perfume—and more."). The motif sprang up on displays, matchboxes, cards, shopping bags, posters, and on the dresses of sales girls.

What is meant by "consistency in art technique"?

Once upon a time, the Pepsi-Cola Company had a problem. Their fine effervescent product came in a bottle that was larger than that of their most important competitor, and it cost the same. It required less than mathematical genius to know that when you bought a bottle of Pepsi you got more drink for the money. Therefore, this cola was cheaper than the other. So was— as to be expected—its image.

Restaurants were reluctant to put a Pepsi-Cola bottle on their customers' tables; they did not want to appear miserly. Hostesses preferred the smaller, more expensive version of the stuff, too; they wanted to display their good manners. To increase its share of the market, Pepsi-Cola set out to change its image. It devised a campaign which was to upgrade their oversized bottle. It acquired the services of some fine artists, used white space lavishly, and made its labels appear cleaner, nicer. Soon, sales began to rise.

The company believed in graphic consistency in advertising. Still following the ground rules, the company decided that a *slight* change in art technique would be a welcome turn of events. The situations—a meeting of two or more highly taste-conscious individuals—remained, but gone was the white space, the sophisticated combination of colors, the delicate brush strokes, the subtleties that only top illustrators recognize. Crudely executed, naïvely drawn illustrations took the place of the old ones.

The result was a drop in readership and noting. Even more detrimental to the company was the assault on its carefully built-up image. Even though the pictures and text told of smart people, the execution belied the premise. For no really definable reason—it is difficult to articulate on the fine points of art—the campaign lost much of its flavor. Soon, Pepsi-Cola corrected the situation. Again, white space came to fore, with clean typography and a smart artistic handling of smart people. The advertising once more became consistent with the corporate image of the Pepsi-Cola Company.

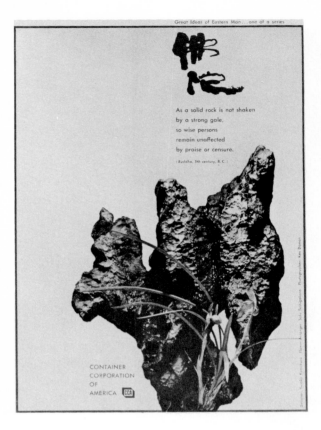

About thirty years ago, the Container Corporation of America was examining *its* corporate image. Its management, with the late Walter Papecke at the lead, concluded that what the company needed was an institutional campaign to end all institutional campaigns. And so the "Great Ideas of Western Man" was born.

This series was to let the buyers of Container Corporation products know that they were dealing with a design-conscious company. It was also hoped that young aspiring artists would become so imbued with the appearance of the ads that they would want to join up. The campaign helped the Container Corporation in achieving both these aims.

Almost every advertisement in this campaign —and there were hundreds of them—was executed by a different artist. Abstract painters made room for photographers, woodcutters for mosaicists, Chinamen for Hungarians, brute males for fragile females, fledgling artists for old-timers, illustrators for typographers. Yet— unlike the Pepsi-Cola campaign—there was "consistency in art technique" throughout every single insertion in the course of three decades. The management of the Container Corporation of America and its able, art-oriented advertising agency, N. W. Ayer & Son, Inc., realized that it is the *spirit* of the campaign that counts.

It is a mistake to think of consistency of art technique in overly rigid terms. Once the basic graphic theme is decided upon, there may be a number of directions the artists (photographers or designers) can take. The typography may change. The layout can be altered. From black-and-white ads it is possible to switch to full-color ones and vice versa. Logotypes can be moved a few inches to the left or right, up or down, and in spite of such "major" changes the ads will still not lose their family resemblance.

This is the important point to decide upon: What is the purpose of the advertising? What is the image the company is attempting to achieve? Don't lock yourself—and the artists you hire for substantial fees—into a homemade box, so small you can hardly move. Lay down *general principles*. Then swing freely.

The corporate image: people, product, or places?

It is safe to say that most manufacturers' favorite picture is that of their own factory. After all, this is where the product is *made;* what could be more dramatic than that? The factory—to the owner at least—becomes a symbol of accomplishment.

There are indications that consumers do not always share the manufacturer's justifiable pride in his property. They often prefer to see the product instead. The people who handle the product—shopkeepers, repair men, salesmen— also occupy an important place in the world of the consumer. He tends to associate them with the company; if he likes them, he likes the company.

A dramatic demonstration of this tendency is gasoline-buying behavior patterns. Here the station attendant plays a primary role. A study made for the *Chicago Tribune* by William Henry revealed the surprising fact that loyalty to a brand is often synonymous with the liking of the station attendant down the block. Cleanliness, efficiency, friendliness were considerations that took precedent over the brand of gasoline.

SEA BREEZE · DESIGNED BY GEORGE THOMPSON · HEIGHT 15 INCHES · $1,250
MADE AT THE CORNING GLASS CENTER · CORNING, NEW YORK

STEUBEN GLASS
FIFTH AVENUE AT 56th STREET · NEW YORK 22, N.Y.

This year give beautiful legs

Chemstrand nylon

Distinctive art treatment can be of substantial help in building an image.

The photographic illustrations used by Steuben Glass accurately convey the feelings the company has about its own product—no explanation is necessary. The stark simplicity of composition, the use of dramatic lighting, the restrained layout and typography, and, most of all, the willingness to show only one (or possibly two) items in a full-page advertisement give this campaign lasting impact.

The Chemstrand campaign has given nylon its deserved sophistication. It turned nylon stockings from a utility to a luxury item; it made the women who wear them feel *smart*. Sensitive photography, colorful layouts, and a unique, exciting graphic idea in every single ad helped to create the image. The pictures have an aura of chicanery so essential to impressing women.

Good things begin to happen...
when the lady of the house has soup for lunch

Have you had your soup today? *Campbell's*, of course!

The Columbia Broadcasting System is in the process of carving out an image distinctively its own. Of all the major networks, CBS appears—to the general public—to be the most progressive and up to date. Programming and choice of personnel of course are important factors in developing this image. But so is the consistently excellent—and modern—graphic treatment used in all advertising, promotional material, titles.

Knowing exactly why people like soup, Campbell's set out to build just the right image for its product. For years, with astonishing regularity, the company has bought full-page magazine ads and television spots all expressing the same idea: Soup tastes good. Pictures radiate the simple joy of having a warm bowl of soup at home.

Wherever you go...go first by Long Distance

"*I always call ahead. Doesn't everybody?*"

"Really it's Daddy who calls and asks for reservations. Then we pack up and go."

No doubt about it—calling ahead for reservations is a good idea. For you, too.

BELL TELEPHONE SYSTEM

Betty Furness did for Westinghouse what Uncle Sam has done for the United States. She became a symbol of the company. With the aid of her straightforward, unassuming, and disarmingly honest manner, she has sold thousands of appliances. Not only do housewives associate themselves with what she represents (the glamorous but still down-to-earth housewife) but so do Westinghouse dealers (an important consideration for the company).

One of the most remarkable case histories of successful image developing is that of the Bell Telephone System. Many people think of this corporation as they would a public institution. Though the dividends paid by AT&T would indicate that financial problems have never been among the most pressing ones, the average person still likes to think of the "telephone company" as one that puts service above profit making. AT&T advertising helps in forming this attitude.

The Volkswagen campaign created history not only in the advertising world but also in the automobile industry. Ads received exceptionally high readership (even for automobile advertising), and cars sold by the millions. This campaign also has a distinctive art technique, though not apparent at first glance. Layout and photography are so simple, so utterly devoid of any advertising gimmickry, that the "lack" of technique actually becomes a technique. Unlike some of Detroit advertising, all Volkswagen ads make a single graphic statement.

Very different but also effective was the campaign authored by the Renault company. Effort was made here to build a distinctive image of the car. In this the advertisers succeeded. With the help of colorful typography (cluttered but carefully designed), the mixture of French and English text, the ever-present symbol of gaiety, and the red-white-blue balloon threesome all connote the idea that Renault is a car for those who drive for enjoyment.

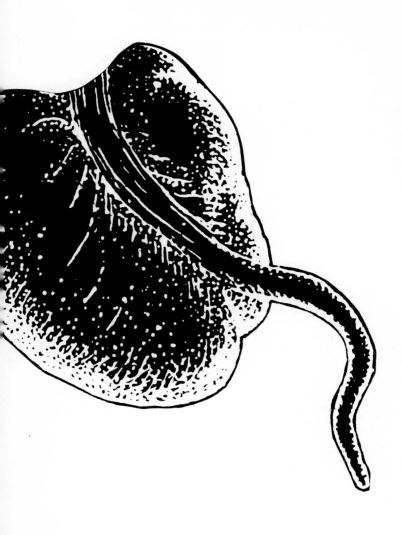

APPENDIX

A few comments (some controversial)
on industry's failure to use
"visual persuasion" to its fullest advantage

One of the most remarkable phenomena of American business—supposedly the most sales-minded in the world—is its failure to realize the inherent power of visual communication.

Just as the man-on-the-street, the average business executive, even though more knowing about the chicanery of persuasion, is apt to think of communication in terms of the *verbal*. He, too, wants his story to be "spelled out." He, too, professional as he may be in his field, earnestly believes that *direct* communication is always superior to the *implied*. At the same time, he will bring flowers to his wife to tell her of his love, wear his best suit to a business meeting, and otherwise use the subtle means of implied communication in his private life a hundred times a day.

Why is it that those in mass selling—in advertising—fancy that the people who buy the goods are any different from their wives, children, or friends they know so well? Says Ernest Dichter, a man who spent many years exploring the hidden crevices of the human mind: "There is much evidence to show that it is the nonverbal, implied communication, that is often more effective than the logical verbal form of communication."

Badly needed in industries are men who are visual-minded.

There are usually a number of highly skilled articulators in every company. They may be found in advertising departments, in public relations, in the area of middle management, or—most often—at the very top. It is no secret that some of the most potent writers and speakers are those who govern the fate of the company. Many of them have the talent to plot novels, conceive plays, engage in business correspondence and memo writing, the powerful phraseology of which would amaze even the most literary-minded. Few can produce advertising copy as convincingly as these professional wordsmen. And even more of them are capable of acting as constructive and incisive critics.

This is not the case when it comes to pictures. Business executives often share the feelings of the general populace in regard to art. They are skeptical of its worth. The subtleties that give paintings emotional undertones befuddle them. Typical is the letter a top business executive sent to *Fortune* regarding its use of illustrative material:

It occurred to me after reading several of the recent issues of *Fortune* that you are following a policy that may not serve your reader's interest as well as you think. The practice I have in mind is the use of semi-abstract illustrations with some of your industrial articles. I noticed that you used the technique in "The Mighty Shapes of Vision."

The sketches are indeed colorful; alas, that much can be said for them. One senses the frustrating sensation of searching for details that plainly don't exist. The articulate mind and eye may enjoy the feeling and brief impression. If he is what your promotional literature says he is, then maybe this technique should be reconsidered.

I'm not a severe critic of the type of illustration you've employed here. I can't help wondering, however, if your choice of this form of illustration on these subjects is not defeating your purpose. If your purpose is to inform, I think these illustrations generally fail. . . .

Perhaps you've chosen this as a happy union of art and industry. I still can't help but wonder if the employment of better photographers with a touch for the dramatic and more fertile imagination wouldn't be a better vehicle for illustrations.

Expressed in this piece of correspondence is a sincere plea for realism. The assumption is that representational art is the most cogent of visual communication. In many respects, this is true (see Chapter 1 on "The Peculiar Taste of the American Public"), but like most generalities it holds many dangers. The implication is, in effect, that a detailed rendition of a subject is the *only* pictorial form which can explain an idea.

While every professional visual persuader worth his salt will agree that a message must get through to the reader (or, in this case, the viewer) in order to make him act upon it, he will not concede that absolute realism—as understood by the visually untrained mind—is the only *modus operandi*. Such rigid theories leave little opportunity for creative artists to conceive distinctive—and possibly more effective—means of visual communication.

Compounding the confusion industrialists

often feel about art is their general attitude about the artists themselves. The most widely held point of view is that, while businessmen have their feet firmly planted on terra firma, artists spend most of their time traveling in orbit. This gives most executives, who are held responsible for misuse of funds, a sense of alarm, if not panic. Plainly they do not know what to make of the creature waving a piece of paper full of funny marks in front of them.

There should be men in industries who understand art. This does not mean that every corporation should have artists on their staff. It does not even necessitate the employment of personnel who have taken a night course in art and have become, as if by magic, authorities on all matters pertaining to the visual. Required is the presence of an intelligent, open-minded, and artistically unprejudiced individual who can work with artists without their going to the window, opening it, and with a magnificent gesture putting an end to all their problems forever.

What to tell an artist.

Familiar are the murmurs emanating from certain offices "that artists are unable to comprehend their clients' problems." They are, so the buyers of art claim, apt to "misinterpret" instructions.

There are often good reasons for the complaint. Artists, too, can be inarticulate in getting their points across. More often than not, their schooling provides them with little background to cope with the everyday problems of business life. And frequently they are the most ardent snobs of all; they mistrust business more than business mistrusts them, and the result is usually a complete breakdown of communication between the two camps.

Nevertheless there is strong evidence that it is not always the fault of the artist that after the work has been delivered to the buyer he is left in a state of shock. The instructions given are often either too vague or—and this also can mar the quality of the output—overly confining. For example:

A food company in Texas requested an estimate, "as accurate as possible," from a package firm for the designing of a carton (as they described it) to "accommodate six of our cans." The sizes of the cans were not given. Also kept secret were quantity of boxes needed, the approximate message that should appear on them, and the nature of the product.

A sculptor was asked to submit sketches for his ideas in decorating a large reception room. In order "not to hamper his creative urges," he was not permitted to see the foyer. Result: a design for a fountain larger than the entire reception room.

A manufacturer of matches wanted a new, "modernized" version of his old box, "beautiful enough to fit into the décor of a living room." The following specifics were among the instructions as to what should appear on the package: a picture of the site of his handsomely landscaped factory, a description of the quality of matches in the box, and a "2 for the price of 1" introductory offer. Inevitably the outcome was a hodgepodge design of a package too homely even to put in a bathroom.

A vice president of an industrial corporation called in several top designers to find a trade symbol that would look very much like that of its parent company ("Their reputation is money in the bank for us") yet totally different ("We don't want people to think that we are not an independent organization").

A photographer was assigned to take a picture of an automobile "moving so fast one could hardly see it," but at the same time he was to make sure the new grille was clearly visible.

An art director was handed the problem of laying out a "big-picture" newspaper ad. The text, even set in small type, took up over three quarters of the available space.

A dog-food manufacturer was wondering if his agency could prepare a two-minute television commercial to "incorporate everything that has ever been said about this type of product" so he could be the proud possessor of "the end of all dog-food commercials." He got it. It left the audience in a complete state of uncertainty as to the identity of the sponsor.

Hit-or-miss assignment of problems? Yes, instructions of this kind represent just that. They cause delay, waste of money, fraying of temperaments. Yet dealings like that are not as infrequent as one—basing his conclusions on the intelligence of the people involved—would imagine them to be.

Actually, artists are primarily interested in defining their problems in two respects only:

1. They want to know the production requirements (number of colors, size, reproduction methods).

2. They want to know the *purpose* of their assignment. They do not relish being told *how* a job should be executed, but they do welcome information on *what* the advertiser wants to convey (image of the company, type of audience to be reached).

Scribbles or "comps"?

A favorite pastime of business people is to view comprehensive sketches of things to come. Like everyone else, members of various management teams *like* to look at pictures; such presentations usually involve more showmanship than just routine reports made by, let's say, an accounting department.

There is of course nothing wrong with passing the time away in this fashion. An examination of tightly rendered art recommendations prevents the participants from laying a giant egg at a later date—an event that could cost the company several thousand dollars. The artist, too, is assuming a lesser risk if his sketches are approved in as "finalized" a form as possible before finished art is prepared.

There is evidence, however, that the custom of "buying art" just from looking at carefully worked-out layouts before anything more has been done with them is not always the best practice. Quality often suffers. And frequently the costs are higher. Skillfully rendered recommendations are often particularly impressive to the layman (and most businessmen belong in this category) who likes to state, half apologetically and half proudly, that he "cannot draw a straight line." Thus the professional sketch man who wields pastels and brushes with a sleight of hand has in his power the means to make a profound impression on his audience. His ability to draw pretty girls prettier than ever before, portray a landscape with "that three-dimensional feeling," make an automobile look sleeker and glossier than could be imagined possible can make those who "okay" art nod approvingly.

Art studios, advertising agencies, industrial designers are well aware of this very human tendency on the part of business management. Almost all employ well-paid sketch men who can "put it on paper" for the benefit of those who like to buy only what is in front of them.

It is easy to see why, at times, too meticulous a rendering of ideas can do more harm than good in the long run. In the first place, the glitter of presentation may hide the lack of a sound, original picture *concept*. The girl in the layout may be the most beautiful that ever came out of a paintbox, but after all is said and done, she is still only one of many pretty girls who would appear in thousands of other advertisements. In layouts, what she does, the reasons for her being there, should be more important —and studied with more care—than the art technique that makes her look so impressive. The artistic talent should get primary consideration *after* the basic concept is analyzed, not before.

In the second place, tight renderings done by staff artists usually prevent an outside talent— photographer, designer, or illustrator—from making significant contributions of his own. Once the comprehensive sketch has been approved by top business management, there is little opportunity to change the picture.

More and more advertising agencies and other idea-producing institutions are educating their clients in visualizing picture concepts from the roughest form of renderings. One of the largest agencies in the world, Young & Rubicam, "sells" advertising ideas by means of an art director's loose sketches. A young and up-and-coming agency, Koenig, Papert & Lois, reputed for its creative sparkle, also makes it a rule to "talk" visuals from casual pencil jottings of their art department. In their dealings with artists and photographers, magazine art directors—some of the most brilliant in the field—very rarely use tightly rendered layouts. Picture concepts are decided upon on the basis of thumbnail sketches, sometimes only on the back of envelopes.

The limitation that handsome but overly exact renderings impose on the people who must execute ideas after they have been approved is especially prominent in the television industry. Tight storyboards that give the client a blow-by-blow description of what he is going to see on the screen cause production costs to skyrocket with no apparent improvement in quality. The changes invariably suggested during the shooting schedule—such as rearrangement of scenery, addition or elimination of backgrounds, faster cutting, or optical devices that will ensure smoother transitions between scenes—are not ideal for keeping peace in the multitudinous family of business executives who have already seen and approved the storyboard. "Do not tinker with the okayed commercial" becomes the motto even though a bit of "tinkering" would be best for all concerned, including the client.

There are, of course, many clients who insist on a polished visual presentation. After all, there are great expenses involved in approving advertising concepts. Why make decisions on the basis of "pig-in-the-poke" showings? When the buyer of art feels he is entitled to seeing something closely resembling the finished product, the proposer might consider the possibility of showing just that. But again, comprehensive layouts are not always the cure-all (they might be, but not in *every* case). It is possible that the artists, photographers, designers, and television producers who eventually would be assigned the finished job might be asked to help make up the presentation. The majority of photographers are willing to take pictures on an experimental basis, for a fee that later would be absorbed in the costs anyway. Artists too are usually delighted to submit their own interpretations instead of having to adhere slavishly to someone else's "already approved" sketch. To hire designers to copy someone else's design to the letter is also a waste of good money. And television producers welcome the opportunity to work on storyboards with advertising agencies *before* rigid picture ideas are submitted to the client.

Admittedly, such presentations incur some costs, possibly more than those of a routine agency showing of comprehensive layouts (most agencies charge nothing for even the tightest renderings; the preparation of layouts falls in the category of "creative services"), but they take maximum advantage of everyone's talent before it is too late.

Not every presentation has to be this elab-

orate. The "other" kind—that of making decisions from the art director's scribbles—can be just as fruitful. However, in this case the client should keep in mind that art directors are hired primarily on the basis of two functions:

1. *Creative ability.* Strong ideas make consumers buy a product. When sizing up an art director's layouts, look for advertising *ideas,* not for superficial visual gimmicks.

2. *Ability to buy art.* The polish of execution will largely depend on the men and women who are assigned to do the "finish." It is the art director—his taste, experience, and advertising sense—who finds the right talent to execute ideas. Form an opinion of his *judgment,* not his craftsmanship.

How to appraise a visual concept.

Advertisers like to demand proof positive on every suggestion submitted to them, be it a marketing plan, a copy platform, or a piece of art.

In principle, this is a fine idea. An increasingly larger portion of total expenditures is devoted to sales and advertising. To spend great sums of money on the hunches of a few would be asking too much of management. In the past, advertising—and everything that went with it—had been performed in a casual manner that indeed disheartened those who believed in the virtues of efficiency in business.

Yet, there is reason to believe that visual selling is still largely a matter of instinct. To be sure, research can unearth valuable *information.* This book is packed with pictures which suddenly took on new meanings from the findings of motivational and readership reports. It is doubtful, however, whether all these pictures were conceived by analytical minds. Many were created by inspired minds. It is one of the peculiarities of artistically intuitive men and women that they should also be psychologically in tune with their fellow beings around them. Many of Freud's precepts have been forecast by great novelists, playwrights, and artists who had never taken a course in psychology. Nonetheless, their works—as are the illustrators' and photographers' works represented in the pages of this book—were psychologically sound.

No meeting groups—even the largest—will ever take the place of the minds of a few sensitive individuals who bring home the ideas. Those skilled in oratory may be able to explain ideas, ridicule them, sell them, and make them go away, but in the end it is not always the articulator who spells out progress.

Research, group meetings, reassuring as they may be, do not prevent mistakes from being made. They merely divide responsibility.

At the present time, because of the increased availability of factual information, the instinctive approach to visual selling is thrown into the background.

Don't let this happen. It just isn't sound business procedure.